ROB MADGE

Rob Madge is a theatre-maker, writer, actor and all-round ~ of campness from the middle-of-nowhere in the Midlands.

They began working professionally in theatre at the age of 9, having spent the majority of their childhood forcing their family to help them put on shows in the living room.

Theatre roles as a precocious child actor include Michael Banks in *Mary Poppins* (Prince Edward Theatre), Fleance in *Macbeth* (Gielgud Theatre), Artful Dodger in *Oliver!* (Theatre Royal, Drury Lane), Gavroche in *Les Misérables* (25th Anniversary international tour and concert), Reginald in *Matilda the Musical* (Courtyard Theatre, RSC).

Theatre roles as a grown-up-but-probably-still-precocious actor include Ensemble in *Les Misérables* (UK and international tour – yes, they did it again), *Timpson the Musical*, *Held Momentarily, Leave a Light On*, *Roles We'll Never Play*.

In between doing *Les Mis* as a child and as an adult, Rob studied English Literature at the University of Warwick, but really spent the majority of their time being involved in (and eventually being President of) the musical theatre society. Typical. Following this, they graduated with a Master's in Musical Theatre from the Royal Academy of Music, being awarded the DipRAM.

Rob is determined to spread queer joy across stages and celebrate all that makes us really quite wonderful things.

In their spare time, Rob enjoys Ben & Jerry's Cookie Dough and watching repeats of *Don't Tell the Bride*.

Twitter: @rob_madge_02
Instagram: robmadge02
TikTok: rob_madge_

Other Titles in this Series

MY SON'S A QUEER (BUT WHAT CAN YOU DO?)

A play by Rob Madge

With lyrics by Rob Madge and Pippa Cleary

Foreword by Luke Sheppard

Afterword by Jon & Jan Madge

*And additional material from
the RDM Productions Archive*

NICK HERN BOOKS

London

www.nickhernbooks.co.uk

A Nick Hern Book

My Son's a Queer (But What Can You Do?) first published in Great Britain in
2020 as a paperback original by Nick Hern Books Limited, The Glasshouse, 49a
Goldhawk Road, London W12 8QP

Cover artwork by Harry Neal Creative
Designed and typeset by Nick Hern Books, London

Printed in Great Britain by Mimeo Ltd, Huntingdon, Cambridgeshire
PE29 6XX

A CIP catalogue record for this book is available from the British Library

ISBN 978 1 83904 012 2

Contents

RDM Productions Proudly Present

CINDERELLA

This show is on Wednesday 24th December 2003 Christmas Eve

Written by Robert Madge
Directed by Robert Madge

Programme

'Everyone, this was the programme!'
(Courtesy of Word Art)

Welcome

Ladies and gentlemen, boys and girls welcome to tonight's fabulous performance of '101 Dalmatians'. A lot of effort has gone into this so we hope you very much enjoy it.

To make a fantastic show you obviously need a brilliant cast and crew. Yes, we only have two but they're both still extraordinary! We would firstly like to thank Jon Madge for his good ideas for the set (which we never used in the end) and his commitment (wink, wink, nudge, nudge) to the show. Our ultimate thanks goes to the brilliant Robert Madge who did all the research, all the writing, all the creativity for this show. If he wasn't involved the show would be incredibly lacklustre and down right crap. Remember that show dad did on his own???

Now, ladies and gentlemen it's time for you to settle down in your seats and relax as we present before you '101 Dalmatians'.

Yours sincerely,

The amazing Robert Madge (I am modest aren't I?)

101 Dalmatians

Welcome to our show!

Good evening ladies and gentlemen and welcome to the fabulous show of 'Rags to Riches: The Story of Cinderella'. It features award winning music from two of the highest acclaimed composers – Rogers and Hammerstein who also wrote the fantastic musical 'The Sound of Music'.

We would like to say a big thank you to all our guest stars for flying over from cartoon land/fairy land to be with us today. Unfortunately the Disney Fairy Godmother is unable to attend today but I think you'll find we have got the perfect replacement!

It isn't all just actors this, actors that though... oh no! When you're sitting down with your cup of tea and enjoying what happens in front of you, a lot more stuff goes backstage then on. Thank you sooo much Robert Madge who makes this a truly dazzling show. He manages to perform everything himself. Lights, scenery, props, costumes, orchestra and performers. Wow!

So, anyway, we hope you all enjoy the show! It's a hit!

Jon Madge
(Theatre Owner)

Cinderella (safe to say, this was not, in fact, written by Jon Madge)

Foreword
Luke Sheppard

Queer. Like so many others, that word haunted me in the playground. I never really knew what it meant, but I knew it was something that made me different, that it was something people could see in me, even if I had no idea what it was they were even looking for. I thought I was alone. Of course – how wrong I was.

As I distanced myself from those who would use that word against me, I found myself drawn closer and closer to a world where the things that made me different were celebrated. In short, I found the theatre, and with it, a community of people who let me be... well, me.

It didn't matter that I couldn't really sing, or that I couldn't land a double pirouette, or that I never got a look-in for the lead roles. All that mattered was that I was a part of it. And so when I stumbled across Rob's story on social media, I recognised it immediately. That was me. And I know many others would have felt the same, for as I grew up I came to understand that mine and Rob's experience had been repeated in every corner of the country. Although, it must be said, I think Rob lived their story with particular flair and style.

In fact, I had already met Rob, but it had been when they were a child performer in *Matilda the Musical* at the RSC. I was the fresh-faced Assistant Director who had just graduated from university, and part of my job was to make sure all the young company were fully rehearsed. It was quite a task. Luckily I have a distinct memory that Rob knew the show better than I did, and they were the complete perfectionist. I also remember that nothing stood between them and their stage. Even at the time I thought it was amazing.

So really it is no surprise at all that a decade later they have written this extraordinary new play. And it is extraordinary, for while the spotlight might have been Rob's destiny, I am reminded it takes a special bravery to make a one-person show. And I'd like to thank Rob for their honesty and trust in telling this story, and for giving it to us to share. This is Rob's story after all, even if so many of us can see glimmers of ourselves within it.

And so I come back to that word...

Queer. Like Rob, and like so many others, no longer do I run and hide from it, I celebrate it. And I believe that is what this play is about: a story of hope for all those young people who find themselves creating their own one-person show when they feel there's no role in the world around them. To all those who would rather be putting on their own Disney parade in their living room than playing football, even if that makes them, well... completely, utterly and brilliantly queer.

But importantly, this play is also for another key audience too. It's for the grown-ups. The mums, dads and guardians who are also maybe just a bit scared of that word. Don't be. Because after all – what can you do? Well, it turns out: quite a lot.

On that note, I will leave Rob's words to do the talking. Enjoy the play!

My first job.

Robert wins role in Mary Poppins

Robert Madge, 9, has begun the role of Michael Banks in the London musical Mary Poppins. Michael is one of the children whose lives are changed by the magical nanny. Robert was competing with boys who'd already won leads in West End shows. He rehearsed for a month, looked after by a chaperone away from home, and plays at the Prince Edward theatre until May 2006.

Stagecoach Tamworth

Madge began acting when he was 4, after a family trip to Disney World. "When we got back, I was always pretending to be Peter Pan at home," he said. "And that was where I started acting. I know every kid does that. Every kid dresses up and pretends to be a Disney character, but for me, I actually stood back and realized this was what I wanted to do."

Introduction
Rob Madge

I put on shows in my living room and now I'm putting on a show about it.

In 2020, I began sharing old home videos of shows I would put on in the living room as a child. Anyone that works in or loves theatre knows that the living-room shows are a rite of passage. I shared them because I thought they were funny and daft and bizarre. They are all these things. What struck me, however, and what I wasn't necessarily expecting, was how they resonated with people for one reason or another, be that because it made them miss their childhood, made them miss the innocent magic that made them fall in love with theatre in the first place, or simply made them feel good. One thing was clear: people were nostalgic.

What also became clear was that my upbringing is not necessarily the norm. I received many messages saying how lucky I was, that their family would not indulge them so, that their dad would never have let their son wear a wig, let alone be seen dead wearing one himself. I knew then that my family deserved a tribute and I needed to let those families that aren't so confident in letting their son play Ariel know that it doesn't have to be some scary, other-worldly thing. It can be hilarious and chaotic and beautiful and uplifting and pretty easy.

I had a debate with someone about whether or not we need to draw attention to the queerness of it all, whether it's relevant or not, seeing as I was a child at the time. However, visibility is everything. At the time, it was just a wig. Now, looking back and knowing I am who I am today because of the supportive environment in which I was raised, the wig means more, especially knowing some parents wouldn't permit it. More so, the notion that a joyful, funny show ought not to address queerness irked me. It implied that queerness is in a sort of opposition to innocence and fun and joy. So often the only queer stories we see are those that are rooted in trauma. That is not to deny the importance of these stories, nor am I suggesting they should not be acknowledged. They are vital. However, we also desperately need to offer an alternative.

I firmly believe it's time to see these stories that are uplifting and funny and entertaining and, yes, abundantly queer. We need to show that raising a flamboyant son with love can blossom into fierceness, pride and self-acceptance. And all of it starts in your living room.

From the Madge family to yours, throw on a woollen wig and have a laugh.

x

The Little Mermaid biographies, after I decided to play Ursula as well.

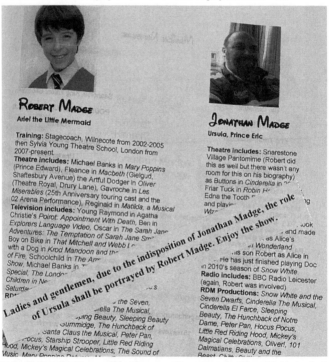

ROBERT MADGE

Ariel the Little Mermaid

Training: Stagecoach, Wilnecote from 2002-2005 then Sylvia Young Theatre School, London from 2007-present.

Theatre includes: Michael Banks in *Mary Poppins* (Prince Edward), Fleance in *Macbeth* (Gielgud, Shaftesbury Avenue) the Artful Dodger in *Oliver* (Theatre Royal, Drury Lane), Gavroche in *Les Miserables* (25th Anniversary touring cast and the O2 Arena Performance), Reginald in *Matilda, a Musical*

Television includes: Young Raymond in Agatha Christie's *Poirot: Appointment With Death*, Ben in *Explorers Language Video*, Oscar in *The Sarah Jane Adventures: The Temptation of Sarah Jane Sm~* Boy on Bike in *That Mitchell and Webb L~* with a Dog in *Krod Mandoon and th~* of Fire, Schoolchild in *The A~* Show, Michael Banks in *~* Special, *The Londo~* Children in *N~* Saturda~ RD~

Ladies and gentlemen, due to the indisposition of Jonathan Madge, the role of Ursula shall be portrayed by Robert Madge. Enjoy the show.

~ the Seven, ~ella The Musical, ~ing Beauty, Sleeping Beauty ~ummidge, The Hunchback of , ~anta Claus the Musical, Peter Pan, ~ocus, Starship Strooper, Little Red Riding ~ood, Mickey's Magical Celebrations, The Sound of Music Mary Ponning D-L

JONATHAN MADGE

Ursula, Prince Eric

Theatre includes: Snarestone Village Pantomime (Robert did this as well but there wasn't any room for this on his biography) as Buttons in *Cinderella* in ~~ Friar Tuck in *Robin H~* Edna the Tooth ~ and playin~ W7~ ~ook ~ and made ~ Wonderland ~t *Wonderland* ~as Alice's ~is son Robert as Alice in ~ He has just finished playing Doc in 2010's season of *Snow White*.

Radio includes: BBC Radio Leicester (again, Robert was involved)

RDM Productions: Snow White and the Seven Dwarfs, Cinderella The Musical, Cinderella El Farce, Sleeping Beauty, The Hunchback of Notre Dame, Peter Pan, Hocus Pocus, Little Red Riding Hood, Mickey's Magical Celebrations, Oliver!, 101 Dalmatians, Beauty and the Beast Cl~

Note: 'Robert did this as well but there wasn't any room for this on his biography.'

Acknowledgements

Firstly, huge thanks to Paul Taylor-Mills and Luke Sheppard for believing in this story. I can think of no greater team to help tell it. Ryan Dawson Laight, you are a genius. George Reeve, thank you for still wanting to do the project even when I sent you practically every home video of my childhood (hefty WeTransfer, that). Pippa Cleary, I don't know what I was doing without you before, to be honest. To all at the Turbine Theatre, thank you for trusting me in putting this story on your stage.

Thank you to Nick Hern Books for making a lifelong goal of mine a reality in publishing the play. Thank you to Russell Smith for your continual support and Helen Mumby for your guidance. To all those at the Royal Academy of Music who reminded me why I fell in love with theatre in the first place, in particular Dan Bowling and Katie Blumenblatt, I owe so much to you. Thank you to all teachers who nurture creativity and encourage students to be bold, unique and fearless, of which I had many, from Stagecoach to Sylvia Young Theatre School.

To friends, old and new, I thank you for your unbelievable support, over the past year especially. To anyone who has enjoyed any of my silly little videos, your encouragement has resulted in this. It's all your fault. My queer family, those I have been introduced to both on and off social media (#GayMis), this is just as much your story as it is mine. To Jaxson and his mother Jennifer, thank you for sharing your experience with me. You are both beacons of hope.

Finally, my family. I'm not quite sure how to thank you all enough. If you fancy being praised any further, have a scroll through my socials. Everyone has already said how wonderful you all are already, but I suppose it bears repeating. My Granny Grimble who I miss with all my heart, thank you for making me Belle dresses and Maleficent gowns, for making pancakes and chicken goujons, for belting 'Silent Night' with a vibrato that would rival Ethel Merman. My nan and grandad, for building me puppet stands and knitting woollen wigs, for crying tears of joy at my performance of a shepherd in the nativity, for eating scones. All my cousins, aunts, uncles, great aunts and great uncles that would perform my scripts with relish on Christmas Eve (I know you all enjoyed it really). My parents. Jon and Jan Madge. Thanks for putting a saucepan on my head one day in 2001 because I wanted a crown like the Evil Queen. You really are to blame for everything. Thank you for raising me to have pride.

And to whoever sold my dad a dodgy VHS player on eBay in 2020, cheers. I've really milked it for all its worth.

R.M.

An early school report.

> ..., Art, Music, Dance
>
> Robert loves playing in the imaginative play area and acting out his favourite stories. He really enjoys listening to stories and looking at books. His drawings of people are quite detailed. He has had opportunities to experiment with colour and texture.

A Stagecoach report, a few years later.

SUBJECT	CONTENT	TEACHER'S REMARKS
DANCE	Rhythm: Good Exercise: Good Effort: Very good Presentation: Good Potential: Good	Robert is currently working on a dance from Grease 'Greased Lightning.' Robert is a quiet member of the group who always works hard and tries his best when dancing. He demonstrates rhythm and nice presentation when dancing. He always tries his best when learning new steps and sequences and tries hard to remember the dance sequences from week to week. Just a little more confidence needed. Keep up the hard work Robert !

The Original Production

My Son's a Queer (But What Can You Do?) was first performed at the Turbine Theatre, London, on 17 June 2021. The cast and creative team was as follows:

MADGE	Rob Madge
Writer	Rob Madge
Lyrics	Rob Madge and Pippa Cleary
Director	Luke Sheppard
Composer	Pippa Cleary
Designer	Ryan Dawson Laight
Lighting Designer	Jai Morjaria
Projection Designer	George Reeve
Sound Designer	Tingying Dong
Video Engineer	Neil McDowell
Orchestrator	Simon Nathan
Mixing	Chris Fry
Sound Assistant	Anna Short
Graphics	Harry Neal
DSM	Rosie Morgan
Sound 1	Nathan Biggs

For the Turbine Theatre	
Artistic Director	Paul Taylor-Mills
Production Co-ordinator	Claire Evans
Theatre Manager	Jimmy Chamberlain
General Manager	Alex Kendal
PR	Emma Holland PR
Social Media Manager	Abby Foster

◀ 'Hello Dad, I'm putting on a puppet show of *Les Mis* today. Here's your cue sheet.'

▼ 'Hello Dad, I'm putting on a show of *Cinderella* today. You're my stage manager. Good luck.' ('No more bubbles.')

At the end they exit cackling. Cinderella is upset and sings a short reprise of 'own little corner' with no music. She exits saying 'I wish I could go to the ball'. Robert clicks 'Impossible' on lyrics and music. He changes into FG costume. The FG enters. Jon operates the bubble gun. She has a few speeches and then says 'You Will Go to the Ball!' She sings Impossible. She exits and this music continues. During this the set changes to the forest. Cinderella later enters in her ballgown outfit. Jon pushes on the chair/carriage and the ornament horse. The bubble machine is still going on. Cinderella sings It's Possible and she rides off to the castle.

The set changes to the castle. No more bubbles. The prince

Everything you could possibly need to put on *The Little Mermaid*.

Christmas is not a time for relaxation.

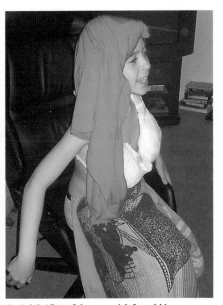

As Ariel: 'Out of the sea, wish I could be… wearing actual wigs and not my Dad's red T-shirt.'

'Ooh, his monstrous appetite!' My first-ever proper costume, The Beast.

'It's actually mine!' The puppet theatre made by Nan and Grandad.

Dad made me a cardboard Chitty Chitty Bang Bang (still the only car I've been able to drive).

Granny Grimble seeing her grandson on a poster at London Euston.

'She's been to Matalan, I do believe.'
Granny Grimble watching me perform *Mary Poppins* whilst wearing all of her clothes.

Me and my mates.

'She made wigs out of wool.'
My first wig, made by Nan.

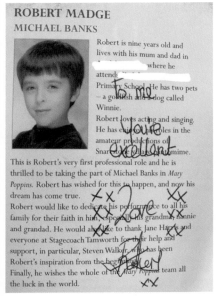

ROBERT MADGE
MICHAEL BANKS

Robert is nine years old and lives with his mum and dad in _____ where he attends _____ Primary School. He has two pets – a goldfish and a dog called Winnie.

Robert loves acting and singing. He has enjoyed roles in the amateur productions of Snow White and Cinderella pantomime.

This is Robert's very first professional role and he is thrilled to be taking the part of Michael Banks in *Mary Poppins*. Robert has wished for this to happen, and now his dream has come true.

Robert would like to dedicate his performance to all his family for their faith in him, especially his grandma Ronnie and grandad. He would also like to thank Jane Harris and everyone at Stagecoach Tamworth for their help and support, in particular, Steven Walker, who has been Robert's inspiration from the beginning. Finally, he wishes the whole of the *Mary Poppins* team all the luck in the world.

Mortified that nobody wanted my autograph at Stage Door, I did one for myself.

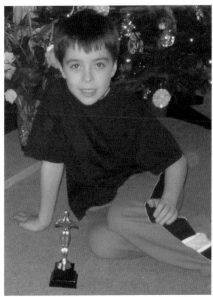

My first Oscar, awarded by Nan and Grandad.

Dad and me as Tooth Fairies in the village panto.

'If it's a bit big, he'll grow into it.' My Maleficent dress, made by my grandma. Dad made the hat.

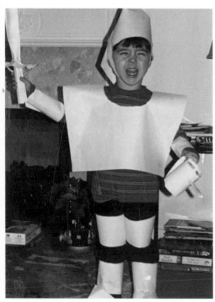

'A love story called *The Wizard of Oz*.'
Dad used a lot of paper to turn me into the Tin Man. A3 as well. What a waste.

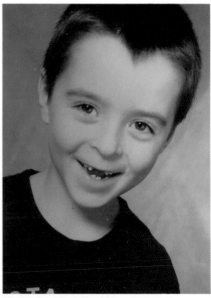

My first headshot. Should have borrowed Granny's dentures.

MY SON'S A QUEER
(BUT WHAT CAN YOU DO?)

Granny Grimble with me in a caravan.

For my Granny Grimble,
who would find the fact she's featured
in a published play absolutely hilarious.
Love you tons x

A Note on the Text

Indented lines indicate video footage.

For example:

    LITTLE BRUMMY CHILD. Welcome to the show.

A line such as this is taken from a video being played on the telly.

This text went to press before the end of rehearsals so may differ slightly from the play as performed.

The space: your living room. A show is about to happen. We see a dusty old telly. Family photos in frames. A fancy-dress box. A big tall thing covered by a dust sheet. Memorabilia scattered around – a home-made Academy Award, a Mary Poppins *chimney-sweep brush. Everything is slightly oversized.*

As the audience filter in –

> *– The dusty old telly shows a video of a young child setting up for a parade – costumes being pre-set, wigs being removed from hairnets, a bubble gun being loaded up with Fairy Liquid. A spectacular production is about to happen. The child addresses the cameraman at one point: 'Yes, Father. I would much appreciate it if you would please put your costume on now.'*

The dad's going to get involved? This is sure to be sensational.

As lights down –

> *– We see the same child appear on the telly screen. A strong Brummy accent.*

LITTLE BRUMMY CHILD. Welcome to the show. Everybody will like this show today and it's a video as well. We hope you like it – um – because it is a bit scary if you're with children but don't matter. Look after them well. Thank you.

We see Madge rehearsing for a living-room spectacular. They address us:

MADGE. Hiya. You'll have to forgive me, you've caught me in the middle of tech. I'm putting on a show in my living room. It's all about my childhood. I know what you're thinking. Yes, it sounds really self-indulgent... Correct.

Song: Anything is Possible (When the Stage is Your Living Room)

CURTAIN UP! THE STAGE IS SET FOR ME
I HAVE GOT A SHOW FOR YOU TO SEE
IT'S REALLY GREAT
IT ISN'T STRAIGHT
COS IT IS ALL ABOUT – WELL – KINDA ME

I'M SO CHUFFED TO BE HERE WITH YOU ALL
EVEN THOUGH THE STAGE IS SORT OF SMALL
WE'LL MAKE IT WORK
I'M HUMBLE AFTER ALL

I DON'T CALL MYSELF A SINGER
Ask my mum
WOW, I PUT HER THROUGH THE RINGER
And then some
BUT NOW IT'S TIME TO SET THE RECORD STRAIGHT
As I said, not straight

ANYTHING IS POSSIBLE WHEN THE STAGE IS YOUR
    LIVING ROOM
ANYTHING IS POSSIBLE WITH UMBRELLAS, A
    SUITCASE AND A BROOM
USE YOUR IMAGINATION
THERE'S MAGIC UP YOUR SLEEVE
(*A flourish*.) Tinker Bell!
YES, ANYTHING IS POSSIBLE
IF YOU JUST BELIEVE

Few months ago, my dad got a VHS player. (*Unveils VHS player, with a flair*.) You remember these, they're the things you used to put cassettes in. Cassettes. No, not Cosette, she's a soprano. 'Why did your dad do this absolutely reckless thing?', you ask. Well, you see, the Madges were feeling very nostalgic and so we rooted through the cupboards, found some dusty cassettes and thought we'd put them to good use.

BACK IN JUNE, WE FOUND A VIDEO
ON A TAPE, VINTAGE, YES, I KNOW
IT'S SORT OF SAD

BUT ME AND DAD
WE PUT ON QUITE THE SHOW!
I say 'we', it was all my idea.
WE HAD PROPS AND COSTUMES, WIGS GALORE
NOW I'M HERE, THE BUDGET'S SHIT BUT SURE
LIKE OLIVER, I'LL LEAVE YOU WANTING MORE
SO JUST THINK OF HAPPY THINGS
Love! Hope!
AND YOU'RE FLYING WITHOUT WINGS
Can you cope?
FOLLOW THE STAR, SOAR AND YOU WILL SEE
THE MAGIC BURSTING OUT OF ME

ANYTHING IS POSSIBLE WHEN THE STAGE IS YOUR
    LIVING ROOM
ANYTHING IS POSSIBLE WITH UMBRELLAS, A
    SUITCASE AND A BROOM
USE YOUR IMAGINATION
THERE'S MAGIC UP YOUR SLEEVE
(*Another flourish.*) Rub the lamp!
YES, ANYTHING IS POSSIBLE
AND THIS, YOU WON'T BELIEVE

In 2009 I was that gay that put on a Disney parade in my hall
for my grandma. I had such high hopes but unfortunately it
went hideously wrong.

Madge inserts a rhinestoned VHS tape into the player.

> *It's a video of them as a child, the same Little Brummy
> Child seen earlier. They are putting on a Disney parade in
> their hall for their grandma, affectionately known as
> Granny Grimble, who is overjoyed at the sight of her
> grandson – sorry – a real-life Disney character at the top
> of the banisters.*

GRANNY GRIMBLE. Mary Poppins!

12-YEAR-OLD MADGE (*dressed as Mary Poppins*). Press
play please.

DAD (*dressed as Bert*). Mary Poppins!

12-YEAR-OLD MADGE. Your cue was 'Oh Bert'.

12-year-old Madge, or 'Mary Poppins', furiously shakes their umbrella. The music should have started by now. 'Mary' attempts to be professional. Smiles through gritted teeth. Joe Public won't clock the show stop. Eventually, the music begins. 'Mary Poppins' slides down the banister and bursts into song. A grand entrance if there ever was one.

12-YEAR-OLD MADGE. ANY DREAM IS POSSIBLE!

12-year-old Madge appears as Mickey Mouse. Their father pushes their float. Or suitcase. Whatever your imagination will stretch to.

GRANNY GRIMBLE. Oh, it's Mickey again!

12-YEAR-OLD MADGE/MICKEY MOUSE. Hiya, folks!

The suitcase has got dodgy wheels. 'Mickey' begins to slide off the already fragile suitcase float. Granny Grimble desperately tries to help.

GRANNY GRIMBLE. Whoops. Whoops. Whoops. Whoops.

The music is coming to an end.

12-YEAR-OLD MADGE. That's one song gone. We should be at the end now…

Dad is dressed as Goofy, attempting to entertain the crowd whilst 12-year-old Madge is embroiled in yet another costume change in the kitchen. He's not doing a very good job. 12-year-old Madge is ready. Dad's not paying attention.

(*Calling from the kitchen.*) Dad! Dad! Dad!

Eventually, Dad hears and comes to assist. The next character appears. 12-year-old Madge is now Ariel, heralded by Dad who holds a cuddly toy fish and furiously blows bubbles from a bubble gun. Clearly, father and son have just had an argument in the kitchen. More cues must have been missed. 'Ariel' makes her entrance on a scooter. The fluidity gives the impression of swimming. Genius, if you ask me. Granny Grimble's impressed too.

GRANNY GRIMBLE. Ooooh!

12-YEAR-OLD MADGE (*to Dad*). Start again.

Dad begrudgingly heads to the office to restart the music on the computer. 'Ariel' strikes a pose. Wishes Dad would get on with it. It's getting awkward. Granny Grimble attempts to cover the pregnant pauses with her enthusiasm.

GRANNY GRIMBLE. Ooh, this is a lovely day. Lovely, lovely day. Beautiful!

12-YEAR-OLD MADGE (*to Dad*). Start again? (*Furiously turns to Mum.*) He doesn't listen to a word I say.

GRANNY GRIMBLE. Come along, Ariel.

12-YEAR-OLD MADGE. I know. That's what I mean – (*To Dad.*) START AGAIN PLEASE.

DAD (*from the office*). I know, I'm trying to. *IT HAS CRASHED.*

Eventually the music restarts. Then crashes. Bad Wi-Fi. Then starts again. 'Ariel' has had enough. Scooters off. Granny Grimble attempts to maintain some calm amongst the chaos.

GRANNY GRIMBLE. She's so graceful. So graceful. Oh so graceful!

The next character appears, this time being pushed on an office chair. These floats have variety. Unfortunately, the office chair can't quite get past the lounge door.

Oh my, goodness me! Watch the floor.

MUM. Ursula!

12-YEAR-OLD MADGE (*dressed as 'Ursula', apparently*). It's me – Aladdin.

Wow. Is my costume really that shit?

Come to a whole new world with me and Jasmine. (*To Dad, who is pushing the office chair in the wrong direction*.) The other way.

The magic carpet gets stuck underneath the wheels of the office chair.

GRANNY GRIMBLE. Oops! You look absolutely –

12-YEAR-OLD MADGE (*dressed as Aladdin*). A WHOLE NEW WORLD.

Time has passed. We see yet another character, yet another costume change. Dad's still on float-pushing duty, but with a Beast mask on this time. 12-year-old Madge now wears a home-made yellow dress and carries a sunflower. It's the best Belle could do for a rose. Black pyjama bottoms sit atop their head. Only the finest quality wigs for Madge.

GRANNY GRIMBLE (*as the office chair attempts to leave the kitchen*). No. It's caught on the bar again.

12-year-old Madge nearly falls off.

Whoops!

12-YEAR-OLD MADGE. ANY DREAM IS POSSIBLE – I'm Belle. This is the Beast.

Nearly falls off again.

GRANNY GRIMBLE. Careful!

12-YEAR-OLD MADGE. SO FIND THE DREAM INSIDE OF YOU… (*To Dad.*) Stay on stage… (*Back in character, furiously.*) I love you, Beast. (*Bursting back into song.*) THERE'S NOTHING YOU CAN'T DO! (*Then, dressed as half of Snow White.*) Snow White is the fairest one of all! I left half the costume in the wrong room…

The parade comes to an end. 12-year-old Madge looks gutted. Crestfallen, in fact. That did not go to plan. Granny Grimble attempts to put a positive spin on things.

GRANNY GRIMBLE. Fabulous, fabulous parade!

Her efforts are in vain.

12-YEAR-OLD MADGE. There was meant to be two more
characters but the costumes went awry.

The video comes to an end. Spotlight on Madge.

MADGE. THAT WAS A TRAGIC TALE
THE SHOW WAS BOUND TO FAIL
BERT MISSED HIS CUE
AND MICKEY MOUSE WAS SUCH A MESS
THE COSTUMES WENT AWRY
AND I SAID 'WHY GOD WHY'
THE FLOAT GOT STUCK, THE BUBBLE GUN BROKE
ARIEL'S BOOBS STRETCHED OUT TO BASINGSTOKE
BUT THAT WAS THEN AND THIS IS NOW
MY NEW TECHNIQUE WILL SHOW YOU HOW
THIS SHINING STAR WILL TAKE THE STAGE BY STORM
AND PERFORM!

YES, ANYTHING IS POSSIBLE WHEN THE STAGE IS
    YOUR LIVING ROOM
ANYTHING IS POSSIBLE WHEN YOUR LIFE IS LIKE A
    DISNEY CARTOON
USE YOUR IMAGINATION
THERE'S MAGIC UP YOUR SLEEVE
(*A final flourish.*) WHEN YOU WISH –
YES, ANYTHING IS POSSIBLE
IF YOU HAVE A COSTUME AND SOME BUBBLES AND A
    SPOTLIGHT AND A SCRIPT
A PYRO, A DIRECTOR – YES, I'M DOING ALL OF IT!
AND THIS PARADE WILL HAVE ITS GRAND REPRIEVE
IF YOU JUST BELIEVE

End of number.

Thank you. I'm thrilled you've all decided to join me on this
most auspicious of occasions, the revival of my Disney parade.
Pause for applause. Thank you. Before we begin, I feel I have to
clarify. This parade was not stand-alone. I insisted we turn the
entire house into Disneyland. You could meet the characters.

We see another video pop up on the telly. The entire house has been transformed into a makeshift Disneyland. Dad is the cameraman.

DAD. Jan, do you want your autograph off Mickey Mouse?

MUM. Yeah.

12-YEAR-OLD MADGE (*dressed as Mickey Mouse*). Oh, would you like an autograph?

DAD. Oh yeah.

MADGE. My grandma rode the teacups.

12-YEAR-OLD MADGE (*pushing their Grandma around their living room on an office chair*). Please put your feet up.

MUM. She'll be sick!

MADGE. Mum learnt to fly with Peter Pan.

12-YEAR-OLD MADGE (*dressed as Peter Pan*). I'm going to teach you to fly.

GRANNY GRIMBLE. Oh for God's sake.

'Peter Pan' flies on a swing in the garden.

MADGE. And Cruella de Vil was dressed in the finest couture.

12-year-old Madge is now Cruella de Vil, adorned in their grandma's dressing gown.

GRANNY GRIMBLE. She's been to Matalan, I do believe.

Madge pauses the video. Turns to us, sheepishly.

MADGE. Yes, I'm an only child. The event was aptly titled 'My Disney World'. And, as you can see, things were running smoothly until I stupidly made the mistake of getting my parents to help with the parade. Pure chaos, all of which could have been easily avoided had my stage manager – sorry – had my dad rehearsed. Had he have taken the Beauty and the Beast float back into the kitchen as opposed to the lounge, Snow White would have had the upper half of her costume. But you know, can't say I'm surprised. He doesn't listen to a word I say.

But that was eleven years ago now. The preview, if you will. And times have changed. I've got some training under my belt. Yes, I'm a very serious actor now. So with that in mind, we're going to have another go at this parade. Now, an important part of my very serious actor process is research. Personal histories, emotional recall, method... and if I don't do this research, the costumes *will* go awry and, quite frankly, I'm better than that now. So, in the words of Connie Fisher, let's start at the very beginning.

Pops a new video in the VCR. Produces magic wand.

Enter my Time-travelling Magic Wand. Oooooh.

Magic Wand, oh Magic Wand
Hear my spell and please respond
Take us back, long ago
To make this parade a spectacular show
Travel through space, past the moon, an eclipse!
Take us to 1996!

We arrive in 1996.

We're there now. It's a short flight. Now, if you want to help your son put on a successful Disney parade, there are seven easy steps to follow. Seven like the sins. Or the wonders of the world. Or Henry VIII's wives and the alternate. Step One: Do not. I repeat. Do not. Throw. A gender-reveal party. Here we are at mine now. It's a familiar scene. Lisa and Gill on the Babycham. 'Live, Laugh, Love' on a cushion. Mum and Dad pop the balloon. (*Pops balloon. A rainbow of colours explode. Madge, in the role of neighbour, looks confused.*) 'But what is it going to be, Jan?!' (*Assumes the role of Mum.*) 'I DON'T KNOW, GILL. THERE IS A MONSTER INSIDE ME!' (*Assumes the role of Dad.*) 'This would never have happened if we'd got a piñata.' So, my parents roll with the first of many a punch and, as such, they take it upon themselves to plaster a rainbow on my bedroom wall.

> *We see a still of Madge's childhood bedroom, a huge rainbow.*

Madge gestures to their outrageous costume.

I blame Mum and Dad entirely. Indoctrination. No but really, they choose to wait and see until I'm born whether my bedroom will be blue or pink so before I make my grand entrance, I'm given a gender-neutral name: Charlie.

> *A video of Dad filming a heavily pregnant Mum balancing the landline on her belly. Will Charlie kick? The tension is palpable!*

DAD. So, Charlie, when you're older and you're watching this video – boy or girl, we still don't know –

MADGE. And we still don't. But even before Charlie's born, one thing is crystal clear.

> GRANNY GRIMBLE. So Charlie is the unseen star of this video then.

MUM. That's it.

> *Mum yawns, disinterested and exhausted. I mean, fair enough. She's very pregnant.*

MADGE. Yeah, cheers, Mum. A few days after this video is taken, Charlie is born in Coventry which is where the *Nativity* films are set so that's lovely. Turns out Charlie has a willy and that matters so Charlie becomes Robert. It's unfortunate but Mum's maiden name was Roberts so I kind of accept the binary purely because of Jan's narcissism. It's a Friday afternoon. The Spice Girls are at number one with 'Wannabe' and Dad makes a remarkably astute observation:

> *We see a video of Madge's grandad holding his newborn baby grandson in the hospital. Dad is narrating from behind the camera, as per usual.*

DAD. You'll be rubbish at football, cricket, but you'll be bloody good in a pub.

GRANDAD. He'll be a proper Madge.

MADGE. And from that moment on, my family see my childhood with one eye closed.

A video montage of Madge's formative years plays on the telly. The transitions between shots are hideously awkward. You know, those dreadful sliding effects. Disgusting. And therefore amazing.

My grandad edited this. Can you tell?

A significant slide.

Get those transitions. Like Alfred Hitchcock, isn't it? I suppose we can say Step Two would be to invest in Final Cut Pro. Now, these are some of my most formative moments.

Baby Madge chilling in a baby bouncer.

Chilling.

The video cuts to a shot of Baby Madge dramatically falling to the ground on a windy beach.

My first death drop... Come on, Cornwall. Let's get sickening!

A video of Baby Madge in a paddling pool with a football.

Ooh, here's me with a football.

Baby Madge looks very confused at said football.

'Excuse me, what is this thing?'

Baby Madge simply cannot get a grasp on the football.

Just doesn't want to be in my hand, does it. No matter how hard I try... Nah, let it go, babe. It's not meant for you. (*Pauses the video.*) Feel I ought to mention. I don't really like football and stuff. I was once asked on stage at the Wolverhampton panto. You know, when Buttons gets the precocious little children in the audience onstage to sing 'Old MacDonald Had a Farm' and be a giraffe. (*Assumes the role of Buttons.*) 'Whey, you're five and now two thousand people are laughing cos you don't know what a giraffe sounds like I HOPE YOU ARE TRAUMATISED... here's the Fairy Godmother with a goody bag.' I'm asked onstage. Buttons turns to me and notices I'm wearing a Leicester Tigers top. They're a rugby team. Never watched the rugby but always liked Princess Jasmine's little pet so the Tigers top suits my purpose. And Buttons turns to me and he goes 'Rugby, ey? What position do you play?' And I respond 'Leicester Tigers.'

The Wolverhampton panto crowd descends into hysterics. Poor little Madge is traumatised.

Honestly, mortifying. And I have to be the giraffe... (*As their 8-year-old self.*) '... Neigh?' But I digress. It's not long before the camera becomes my best friend. Bit like *Fleabag* but without the anal. Yet. I soon develop quite the catchphrase.

> *A video compilation of Madge asking Dad a crucial question over the years. Madge lip-syncs along.*

9-YEAR-OLD MADGE. Are you filming?

> *No response.*

Are you filming?

DAD. No.

> *Mum shoots Dad a look.*

Well, if I say 'yes' then he'll want to stand in front of the lens.

> *9-year-old Madge on a playground.*

9-YEAR-OLD MADGE. Dad.

DAD. Yeah?

9-YEAR-OLD MADGE. Are you filming?

DAD. No.

> *9-year-old Madge on holiday.*

9-YEAR-OLD MADGE. Are you filming?

> *Dad shakes his head. Silence. Madge needs to double-check.*

Are you filming?

> *Another head-shake.*

Tell me when you are.

Something seems suspicious.

Are you filming? (*Sussed it.*) You are, aren't you?!

9-year-old Madge holding an Easter egg, posing for a photo.

Are you filming?

12-year-old Madge at their home-made Disney World, about to push Mum on the teacups.

12-YEAR-OLD MADGE. Are you filming?

9-year-old Madge about to open Christmas presents.

9-YEAR-OLD MADGE. Dad, are you filming?

No response.

DAD, ARE YOU FILMING?!

8-year-old Madge is performing a Christmas concert in their house.

8-YEAR-OLD MADGE. SANTA CLAUS IS COMIN' TO TOWN – (*Aggressively, to Dad.*) *FILM ME* – SANTA CLAUS –

A caravan holiday a few years prior. Dad films Mum, who is reading some romance on a deckchair.

DAD. And here's Janice sat outside the caravan.

Child Madge pops up. How could this content possibly be entertaining?

6-YEAR-OLD MADGE. You're not speaking about me though.

DAD (*exasperated*). And here's Robert.

MADGE. In short, always very shy and retiring. Now, all of the aforementioned is reflected in my school reports, which we know can be quite telling.

Madge blows the cobwebs off a dusty file and rediscovers their old school reports. Over the following, we see stills of the reports.

2001: 'He makes good use of language to imagine and recreate roles.'

2002: 'Robert loves playing in the imaginative play area and acting out his favourite stories.'

2003: 'Robert still enjoys playing in the role-play area and dressing up. He uses scissors and glue carefully.'

2004: 'He *still* loves to be in the role-play area, dressed up as one of his favourite characters.'

> *These reports are typed as opposed to the previous handwritten ones.*

2005: We discover computers. Comic Sans. Classic font. 2005: 'Robert joins in with PE activities although he does not have a great deal of enthusiasm for this area of the curriculum.' Fair. 'The difficulties that Robert had establishing friendships last year...'

Madge is caught off-guard briefly. They spy a broom. A memory stirs.

It's around the time I start school that I become obsessed with *Cinderella*. The definitive *Cinderella*. The 1997 Whitney Houston *Cinderella*. At lunchtime the other kids sprint to the playground to play rounders or try and be Brooke Wyndham with a skipping rope. I choose to stay in the imaginative play area and act out my favourite story.

The broom becomes Cinderella's broom. Madge becomes their 5-year-old self, playing the title role.

Listen, if you haven't seen Brandy as Cinderella... Leave.

Madge gestures to the door for all those who haven't seen Brandy as Cinderella. Honestly, not welcome here. Madge thinks back on the memory and, for a brief moment, seems to lose their sparkle.

Unfortunately, I'm the only one at school who fangirls over Rodgers and Hammerstein. No, I think quite a lot of the others struggle to wrap their heads around a 'boy' that's not into football and stuff.

Madge tries to find more to the memory but it fades. Beat. Remembers they are being watched. The mischievous smile returns. More on that later. For now, back to reality.

Mortified at the sheer consistency of these school reports, Dad tries desperately to find alternative hobbies for me, you know in case being videoed falls through and I need a back-up. He tries museum trips and I'm completely fascinated with the historical artefacts on display.

> *A video of Dad and 4-year-old Madge on a day out at Tamworth Castle. Instead of paying attention to anything remotely historical, 4-year-old Madge is trying on costumes from the dressing-up box. Yes, there was a dressing-up box. Rookie error on Tamworth Castle's part, if you ask me. 4-year-old Madge preens themselves in front of a full-length mirror.*

DAD. You look like, uh –

4-YEAR-OLD MADGE (*hopeful*). Cinderella?

DAD (*not this again*). No. Not Cinderella.

MADGE (*assuming the role of Dad*). 'Jesus Christ. No. Not Cinderella.' (*Sees another father, attempts to reassure.*) 'He's not Cinderella... He goes to Scouts.'

This takes us nicely into Step Two. If you want to help your son put on a successful Disney parade, I have one thing to say:

> *We see a montage of all of Madge's various costumes over the years, the outfits of several Disney princesses all strung together out of bits and bobs around the house.*

Costume. Costume. Costume. Now, I'm not saying you have to outdo the wardrobe of Cher, although it's something I've dabbled in. You can be resourceful. Drag on a dime. We couldn't afford a crown so the Wicked Queen had a saucepan on her head.

We see a still of Madge dressed as Winifred Sanderson.
Her green dress is fashioned out of one of Dad's green
T-shirts. The wig is a cheap tinsel one. I mean, it looks
nothing like Winifred Sanderson.

This is Winifred Sanderson from *Hocus Pocus*. Not convinced
on the wig choice but Bette Midler clearly didn't get hers from
Blackpool Pleasure Beach. Now, hopefully, unless your child is
Agatha Trunchbull, they'll be quite short. It's a trend amongst
children. This means you have artistic licence to dress them up
in your own shirts, so Dad's Oakland Athletics top is
transformed into Winnie's dress. And the beauty of an Oakland
Athletics top is it's really quite versatile.

A still of Madge dressed as Peter Pan, wearing the same
Oakland Athletics top.

Peter Pan. I did have a pair of green pyjama bottoms which I'm
sure Dad would have thought worked better than a dress what
with Peter being the 'boy' who never grew up, not the 'non-
binary', but I justified it as being a tunic.

A still of Madge dressed as the Beast from Beauty and the
Beast.

The Beast. This one's the real deal. Got it at the Disney Store
and everything. Now, all of this high fashion would be nothing
without a runway to showcase it and my chosen runway is my
most favourite of pastimes – the living-room show. Now, this
bit's very important for my research process. If I don't examine
how it went wrong, how will I ever learn how to make this
parade better? Let's start with a tale as old as time.

A video of a living-room production of Beauty and the
Beast *plays. Madge is 6 years old. And the director. And*
the writer. And all-round control freak. Dad is Belle. For
some reason.

DAD/BELLE. Keep trying –

6-YEAR-OLD MADGE. NOOO you don't say that. I told
you...

Cut to 6-year-old Madge dressed as the 'Beast'.

6-YEAR-OLD MADGE/BEAST. I am the Master of this Castle! YOU DO AS I SAY!

DAD/BELLE. I could read you a story?

6-YEAR-OLD MADGE/BEAST. You don't know there's a library yet!

'Belle' goes to speak.

NO, you say something – something else first.

Cut to 'Belle' reading 'Beast' a story.

DAD/BELLE. This is called *Treasure Island*.

6-YEAR-OLD MADGE/BEAST. No, it's called *Beauty and the Beast*.

'Belle' rushes through the story.

DAD/BELLE. Blablablabla…

6-YEAR-OLD MADGE/BEAST. That isn't right!

DAD/BELLE. And they all lived happily ever after.

6-YEAR-OLD MADGE/BEAST. That was not very good.

'Belle' presents 'Beast' with a tea light.

DAD/BELLE. Hello, Lumière.

'Beast' looks at the tea light, nonplussed.

6-YEAR-OLD MADGE/BEAST.…Why's he a candle?

Cut to 'Belle' and 'Beast' waltzing. 'Belle' goes to sing.

No, I do the song!

DAD/BELLE. Go on then.

6-YEAR-OLD MADGE/BEAST. Cos you can't do it. (*Sings.*) TALE AS OLD AS RHYME… No that's not right.

'Belle' tries to speed up proceedings.

DAD/BELLE. BEAUTY AND THE…

'Beast' is unbothered.

6-YEAR-OLD MADGE/BEAST. TALE AS OLD AS TIME…

Cut to Dad and Madge dressed as villagers.

DAD/VILLAGER. We can see him in this magic mirror.

6-YEAR-OLD MADGE/VILLAGER. NOOO Belle shows us that, silly…

Back to 'Belle' and 'Beast'.

DAD/BELLE. That magic mirror is for you.

6-YEAR-OLD MADGE/BEAST. No. You take it. You take it.

DAD/BELLE. No…

6-YEAR-OLD MADGE/BEAST. No, you take it.

'Belle' is confused. This bit wasn't in the script.

NO!!!

Dad as villager again.

DAD/VILLAGER. I've come to take your man to the asylum.

6-YEAR-OLD MADGE. No you don't – You don't shout like that.

DAD/VILLAGER. I have come to take your…

6-YEAR-OLD MADGE. No that's not right.

DAD/VILLAGER. I have come to take your father to the asylum.

6-YEAR-OLD MADGE. No. There's no 'asylum' or 'take'. It's 'I've come to collect your father'.

Dad sighs, exasperated. Resets.

DAD. Take two…

6-YEAR-OLD MADGE. NO IT'S NOT 'TAKE TO'.
HONEST.

MADGE (*pausing the video*). Sidenote to Step Two. Know your
lines. 'Asylum'? 'Take'?! I did feed him the line as well. In one
ear, out the other. Let us not forget: he doesn't listen to a word I
say. We go on. (*Presses play*.)

'Belle' is showing 'Gaston' the Beast in the magic mirror.

DAD/BELLE. He's not a beast. Look.

'Gaston' bursts into the one bit of the song they know.

6-YEAR-OLD MADGE/GASTON. OOH! HIS
MONSTROUS APPETITE!

Beat. 'Belle' is bemused.

DAD/BELLE....His what?

*Cut to 'Gaston' making up the lyrics to the rest of the
song.*

6-YEAR-OLD MADGE. THE MOUNTAINS AND THE
TOWERS, I WILL KILL THE BEAST...

*Cut to the battle scene. 'Beast' slaps 'Villager' with their
paw. 'Beast' dramatically falls to the ground, dead.*

Turn to the hag! Change me back to a prince.

Dad becomes the 'Hag.

DAD/HAG. Magic will come over you...

*'Beast' magically transforms into 'Prince'. 'Belle' goes to
hug 'Prince'.*

6-YEAR-OLD MADGE/PRINCE. Belle – BELLE. No. No
you don't do that. And I say...

'Belle' is still going in for a hug.

Stop it.

The final number.

DAD/BELLE. THE BEAUTY AND THE BEAST –

6-YEAR-OLD MADGE/PRINCE. NO, we have to hold
    hands.

Beauty and the Beast *comes to an end*.

MADGE. I can only apologise for the supporting cast. But
picture this. Only child. Friends, not that many. I'm stuck with
Dad. I can't put the goldfish in drag, you'd never be able to
work a powder puff on those oily scales. So Dad's got no
choice. He has to take part whether he likes it or not.

> *A video from one Christmas morning. It's early. 7-year-
> old Madge is very excited. Dad is very tired.*

7-YEAR-OLD MADGE. WE WISH YOU A MERRY
    CHRISTMAS, WE WISH – Sing... WE WISH YOU A
    MERRY CHRIS– I said sing. Dad. Sing.

Dad gives up and joins in, against his will.

7-YEAR-OLD MADGE *and* DAD. WE WISH YOU A
    MERRY CHRISTMAS. WE WISH YOU A MERRY
    CHRISTMAS –

MADGE. See. No choice. 'SING.' Now, despite all the missed
cues, I'm glad we've gone back to *Beauty and the Beast*
because it's really the bare bones of an RDM Production. That's
the name of my company. It's my initials. It's very raw, very
black-box. But I think it goes to show that sometimes less is
more. Sometimes all an artist needs are his Beast costume and
his –

6-YEAR-OLD MADGE/GASTON. MONSTROUS
    APPETITE!

DAD/BELLE....His what?

MADGE. But this Beast costume is sort of a coming-of-age
moment. Up till this point, I've never had a proper costume
before and, as much as I'd grown to love the Oakland Athletics
top, she is quite the glow-up. Dad buys it for me on a work trip.
Complete surprise. I see the Disney Store bag, race over to it,

'Please be the Belle dress, please be the Belle dress.' (*Sees that it is not, in fact, the Belle dress.*) 'Thank you.' Once I get over my initial disappointment, I put on that Beast's head and it's in that moment that we reach, in the words of Sarah Brightman, the point of no return. 'Attention, parents. Let it be known that I will stop at nothing till I have every prop, every costume, every smoke machine from here to Sandwell and Dudley.' And just like that, our little house in the Midlands slowly begins to transform into the wardrobe department of the London Palladium. It gets to a point where Dad has to google storage units for the expansion of my fancy-dress box. But when we go shopping, there's just nothing about the Princes or the Spidermen or the Beasts that spark my interest. Which is odd because that's the section designed for the boys so surely, they should. So I'm stumped. I know what I want from my living-room spectacular but if that means going over to the pink bit of the shop? My living-room spectacular will have to wait. It's Christmas time. I'm at the Birmingham Hippodrome panto. I see, out of the heavens, the one and only Dame Ria Jones descend from a moon dressed as Maleficent. I am bewitched. She's bedazzled in this dark-purple, huge-collared gown and these horns that, in my eyes, go up to the gods. I know what I need to do. I need to be Maleficent. I drag my parents around every Disney shop, every Primark. Nothing. Pop into Bonmarché. 'Hello, I don't suppose you have any evil-fairy dresses lying about? Well, you ought to improve your stock.' Have a look in Peacocks. Don't even care about going to the pink bit of the shop, it's that important. 'I'm looking for a wicked-sorceress type of look. It's quite a common request.' All my efforts are in vain. Clearly, there's a gap in the market. So, I give up on my Maleficent dream. And then, on Christmas Day, I unwrap this.

A video of Madge unwrapping a home-made Maleficent dress. They rediscover the dress in real time.

DAD. Wow!

MUM. Grandma made that over weeks.

12-YEAR-OLD MADGE (*to Granny Grimble, in disbelief*). You made this?

MUM. She had to keep laying it out on the floor, getting your measurements. It took her weeks.

12-YEAR-OLD MADGE (*to Granny Grimble, still in shock*). You *made* this?

GRANNY GRIMBLE. Your dad made the hat.

MUM. There's a lot of care gone into them.

GRANNY GRIMBLE. If it needs adjusting at all, I'll do it.

MUM. Well, if it's a bit big he'll grow into it.

DAD. That'll fit you till you're about 18.

MADGE. Maleficent is one of the costumes that went awry. She will make an appearance this time.

Grandma, or Granny Grimble as she's known on Equity... 'Grandma' was already taken... she's always hard at work behind the scenes. She knows that whilst I love the Beast outfit, what I really want is to be Belle. I think you can deduce that from my tone when Dad gets to play the role.

A small snippet of Beauty and the Beast *plays again.*

DAD/BELLE. Hello, Father.

6-YEAR-OLD MADGE/BELLE'S FATHER (*grumpily*). Hello, Belle.

MADGE. Wanted his part. So when I decide to put on a Disney parade in my hall, I phone Granny Grimble as I always do at 6.30 p.m., just after *The Weakest Link* (anything before six costs to ring on the landline) and I tell her it's time. It's time to be Belle. So Granny Grimble makes me a yellow dress.

We see the video of 12-year-old Madge in the parade wearing the home-made yellow dress, carrying a sunflower and attempting to get the office-chair float out of the kitchen.

I'd say she's overworked but she brought it all on herself. You see, she accidentally gave me a taster one Christmas.

A video of 6-year-old Madge unwrapping their Christmas present from their Granny Grimble: a colouring book. And a pair of stockings.

DAD. Who's that off?

6-YEAR-OLD MADGE. Grandma.

DAD (*spying the stockings*). What's that? Oh my word.

6-YEAR-OLD MADGE (*holding up the stockings, bewildered*). What's that?

DAD. It's a pair of tights.

GRANNY GRIMBLE. They've got in by accident…

The family scream with laughter. 6-year-old Madge goes to open their next present.

DAD. Might be a pair of knickers in this one.

The memory comes to a close.

MADGE. Step Three: If you want your son to put on a successful Disney parade, I can't stress this enough… Special effects are your friend. A party popper becomes a pyrotechnic, a bubble gun becomes Ariel's grotto, a throw becomes a frontcloth.

A video of a living-room production of Peter Pan *plays.*

6-YEAR-OLD MADGE. ACT ONE.

The throw rises. It's quite a spectacular fire curtain.

Cut to later in the show.

6-YEAR-OLD MADGE. *PETER PAN.* ACT TWO.

The throw rises yet again.

Another point in the show.

6-YEAR-OLD MADGE. *PETER PAN.* THE FINAL ACT.

The throw rises one final time.

MADGE. The technical term for this gauze is the Settee Curtain. It's a crucial part of any production.

If a show does not have the Settee Curtain, one has to ask 'Is there any point doing it in the first place?'

> *A living-room performance of* Hocus Pocus *plays. 6-year-old Madge is dressed in the Winifred Sanderson gear. The show has just come to an end.*

6-YEAR-OLD MADGE/WINIFRED SANDERSON. We didn't have the Settee Curtain.

DAD. It doesn't matter.

MADGE. Doesn't matter? *Doesn't matter?* The devil is in the detail, Jon. You know, Mum and Grandma have paid good money to see my version of *Hocus Pocus*. A full 20p and a Freddo and you think the fact there was no Settee Curtain simply *doesn't matter*. Shocking. Other than that, the production levels are always very advanced. Although Winifred Sanderson might not have a Settee Curtain, she can still fly.

> *More of the living-room production of* Hocus Pocus.

6-YEAR-OLD MADGE/WINIFRED SANDERSON. Drum roll, please… Grandma, watch…

> *Dad hoists 'Winifred' in the air via a tie attached to a broomstick.*

Fly me to Grandma!

GRANNY GRIMBLE. He's gonna be on the stage, isn't he?

6-YEAR-OLD MADGE/WINIFRED SANDERSON. Yes I am.

MADGE. Mystic Meg, my grandma. Now I don't want to spoil the illusion but could anyone tell how that worked? (*The answer is yes.*) Well, you shouldn't have done, so long as the cameraman followed my instructions.

> *6-year-old Madge as Peter Pan:*

6-YEAR-OLD MADGE/PETER PAN. You're not allowed to video Dad. You just video me... Don't video him.

DAD (*getting ready to fly 'Peter' yet again*). I thought we'd already done this once.

6-YEAR-OLD MADGE/PETER PAN. Don't video him, alright?

Mum listens and doesn't video Dad. 'Peter' flies! The tie is used again. No broomstick this time though.

TINKER BELL!

That's Dad's cue.

Drum roll, please...

'Peter' flies.

Drum roll, please.

'Peter' flies again.

Drum roll, please.

Dad looks suitably despondent at being forced to be flyman for the umpteenth time.

We have to fly one more time.

DAD (*worn out*). No.

6-YEAR-OLD MADGE/PETER PAN. Yes!

DAD (*depleted*). No.

6-YEAR-OLD MADGE/PETER PAN. Please.

DAD (*fatigued*). Last one.

6-YEAR-OLD MADGE/PETER PAN. No, I have to fly...

DAD (*almost losing his shit*). Once more then. ONCE more.

6-YEAR-OLD MADGE/PETER PAN. COME ON WE HAVE TO FLY TO NEVER NEVER LAND. QUICK. TINKER BELL. GET PIXIE DUST... (*Realises Dad hasn't got the tie.*) How do we fly?

DAD. Big jump.

> *6-year-old Madge listens to their father and does a 'big jump'. Face-plants into the carpet. Dad drags them off.*

MADGE. And that's what happens when you don't have a tech. I think Dad's still triggered by the words 'Drum roll, please.' It basically translates to 'Why the fuck am I not in the air yet?!' But that face-plant traumatises me. I am determined, from this moment on, that RDM Productions will never replicate such an embarrassing disaster and so I rectify any technical issues in later productions.

> *We see a rehearsal schedule.*

This is my rehearsal schedule for *The Wizard of Oz*. See. Sitzprobe and tech. All accounted for. (*Drawing attention to 24th December.*) And we will NOT be waiting for Santa on Christmas Eve. We will be doing the 'dress rehearsal'. (*And 25th December.*) And we will NOT be celebrating on Christmas Day. We will be having 'notes and clean-up. Et cetera'. And please note: 'A photoshoot for the posters, programmes et cetera will take place on the second day of tech rehearsals – Sunday the 5th of December – during the tea break. Please ensure you are prepared for this.' Dad. I've always liked *The Wizard of Oz*. Probably cos I was sleeping under that rainbow. In fact, to close Step Three, let's have a little bedtime story.

> *We see a video of 4-year-old Madge sat on a treasure chest in their bedroom, telling us a fairy tale. It's very* Jackanory. *Very* CBeebies Bedtime Stories.

4-YEAR-OLD MADGE. I'm going to tell a story. A love story. Called *The Wizard of Oz*. Once they was a girl called Dorothy… Toto, her doggy… (*To Dad, who is behind the camera.*) What?

DAD. Talk properly.

4-YEAR-OLD MADGE. Um… (*Contemplates talking properly.*) It's how I talk – ?!

DAD (*correcting*). Toto, her *dog*.

4-YEAR-OLD MADGE. Toto, her *dog*, um… (*Loses train of thought*.) We see roses. If the roses or not – if the roses or not roses – uh – and she sees the Emerald's Tit – City… So. I'll just take a bow. Uh – at the end but it's not the end yet because I haven't told you about the monkeys… there were some monkeys. 'I'm melting, I'm melting.' And she was dead. Forever. She was like a big blob. The Wizard gets Dorothy back to Kan– (*Hiccups*.) –sas on a balloon but he goes without her. The dog sees a cat and the witch be's dead and that's the end.

DAD. Lovely story.

The video cuts to 4-year-old Madge still sat on the treasure chest, but now dressed as an owl.

4-YEAR-OLD MADGE. I'm an owl.

Beat. Madge takes this in. It's almost getting bizarre.

MADGE. Let's dissect this owl. This owl is not, for the first time ever, my idea. This is all Dad. I'm sitting on that treasure chest, finishing my story and wanting to go and eat my chicken nuggets but no. Dad goes, 'Stop. Stay right there. We have to do this. It's brilliant. It's *brilliant*. We can't possibly wrap until we've got this shot… You are owl.' Bizarre. 'Cut. You are no longer owl. Please return my beanie. Your nuggets are in the lounge.' Clearly, Dad has caught that stagey bug.

The love story called *The Wizard of Oz* is my first venture into the realm of storytelling. My first dip in the pool of writing, I suppose. This soon becomes my true vocation. Never forget when Graham Norton roasts me for it on the BBC.

We see a clip from I'd Do Anything, *the BBC reality show searching for the next Nancy and Oliver. 11-year-old Madge auditioned.*

11-YEAR-OLD MADGE. I write plays and musicals.

THE VOICE OF GRAHAM NORTON. A budding Andrew Lloyd Webber. The Lord had better watch out.

MADGE. Yes, Graham. Yes, he had. From this moment on, I'll always be writing some show or other for the Madges to get their teeth into. I know, I'm so generous. You've met my stage manager – sorry. My dad. You've met my dad... And you might be thinking 'Wow, how lovely that your dad performs your work' which is true, but I'd like to take it a step further. How lovely that my whole family performs my work. Don't applaud them. They have no choice. I now present to you my Christmas production of *Cinderella* starring me, my dad, my mum, my grandma, my auntie, my great auntie, my great uncle, my cousins and my cousin's ex-boyfriend. I'm 7.

> *A Christmas production of* Cinderella *plays. 7-year-old Madge is in full charge of their not-remotely-stagey West Midlands family.*

7-YEAR-OLD MADGE. Everyone ready? Your words are underlined, all of you. We're only rehearsing now. Dad, we're only rehearsing.

MADGE. And this is Step Four: The importance of rehearsal.

7-YEAR-OLD MADGE. Right. Everyone ready? START! Listen. Shush.

> *Granny Grimble is being the classic Granny at Christmas and making sure everyone is fed.*

GRANNY GRIMBLE. Listen, there's loads of food of here. Do you want anything to eat? *Anybody* want anything else to eat?

MUM. Turn the telly off.

> *Auntie Debby sits on the sofa, cup of tea in hand.*

AUNTIE DEBBY. I'm always last on set.

MUM (*to Dad, who is cameraman once again*). Are you videoing everybody holding their scripts?

7-YEAR-OLD MADGE. SHUSH.

> *The show begins. Madge's cousin Lissy plays the title role. She's a teenager. Does not want to be there.*

COUSIN LISSY/CINDERELLA (*mumbles*). 'Oh Papa, I wish I didn't have to do all this housework.'

MUM (*to 7-year-old Madge*). Sit down. We can't see Cinderella.

The camera pans to Madge's great aunt and uncle, Ev and Stan, in their late eighties, scripts in hand, struggling with their reading glasses. They play Mr and Mrs Mouse. Whoever Mr and Mrs Mouse are, I don't know.

GREAT AUNTIE EV/MRS MOUSE. Is it me? 'Oh Cinderella, dear, please come and cheer us up.'

GREAT UNCLE STAN/MR MOUSE (*reads at a snail's pace*). 'Yeah. Come... come on.'

MUM (*to 7-year-old Madge*). Look, your dad can't see Cinderella.

It's Granny Grimble's big moment. She's playing the villain.

GRANNY GRIMBLE/EVIL STEPMOTHER. 'Cinderella, what was all that silly noise?!' (*Proudly.*) I can do that bit good.

Later in the show, another cousin is roped in, Marcus, about 18 years old, broad Walsall accent. He is the Fairy Godmother. Definitely miscast.

COUSIN MARCUS/FAIRY GODMOTHER. 'I'm your Fairy Godmother.'

7-YEAR-OLD MADGE. WAVE YOUR WAND.

Marcus does as he's told and waves an imaginary wand.

COUSIN LISSY/CINDERELLA. 'See you soon, Fairy Godmother.'

COUSIN MARCUS/FAIRY GODMOTHER. Ok. Ta-ra.

7-YEAR-OLD MADGE. You're not on any more.

COUSIN MARCUS/FAIRY GODMOTHER. Good.

Later in the show:

7-YEAR-OLD MADGE. We're cutting out all the songs.

Marcus is back.

COUSIN MARCUS/FAIRY GODMOTHER. 'If you want to go to ball – if you want to go to the ball, go get me four mice, two rats and a pumpkin.'

COUSIN LISSY/CINDERELLA. 'What's a pumpkin, Fairy Godmother?'

COUSIN MARCUS/FAIRY GODMOTHER. 'Well, it's a big round orange thing… Turn these mice into – ' into hoses?

7-YEAR-OLD MADGE. HORSES! Now, you're not on any more so –

COUSIN MARCUS. You said that last time.

7-year-old Madge announces their arrival.

7-YEAR-OLD MADGE. Right. I have to come on now.

GREAT AUNTIE EV. Oh Jesus.

7-YEAR-OLD MADGE/PRINCE CHARMING. 'I'm going to try this slipper on every girl in this kingdom and the one it fits, will be my bride.'

Later, Madge directs Mum and Auntie Debby, who are playing the stepsisters.

7-YEAR-OLD MADGE. You have to stick your tongues out!

And they do.

7-YEAR-OLD MADGE/PRINCE CHARMING. 'May I try this slipper on one of your daughters? Fetch Cinderella.'

GRANNY GRIMBLE/EVIL STEPMOTHER. 'But, Your Highness – '

7-YEAR-OLD MADGE/PRINCE CHARMING. 'I said fetch her!'

We get to a confusing bit of the script. Both Stepmother and stepsisters are supposed to say a line at the same time. Stepmother is premature in her delivery.

GRANNY GRIMBLE/EVIL STEPMOTHER. 'Nooo.'

7-YEAR-OLD MADGE. No. NO YOU DON'T SAY THAT. You have to all say that together.

MUM *and* AUNTIE DEBBY/STEPSISTERS. 'Noooo.'

Stepmother is now delayed in her delivery. Beat.

GRANNY GRIMBLE/EVIL STEPMOTHER. '...Nooo.'

The end of the show.

7-YEAR-OLD MADGE. We come and bow. Come on.

All bow. But it's not over yet! Much to everyone's disdain.

For being a great actor, we're giving out certificates!

EVERYONE ELSE (*a half-hearted cheer*). Wheyyy...

The certificates have all been handed out.

DAD. Don't I get one?!

7-YEAR-OLD MADGE. No. Cos you had a very small part.

DAD. Thanks for that, Rob.

7-year-old Madge proudly displays the programme, made with WordArt.

7-YEAR-OLD MADGE. Everyone, this was the programme!

GRANNY GRIMBLE. Are we going to have some presents?

7-YEAR-OLD MADGE. We have that after the real show. Now we do the real –

COUSIN LISSY. The *real* – ?!

General uproar.

DAD. That *is* the real show! That *was* it! We're not going through all that again!

MUM. No. We're not doing it all again!

GRANNY GRIMBLE. We're going to have some presents now.

7-year-old Madge goes to answer back. Thinks better of it. It's a lost cause at this point.

7-YEAR-OLD MADGE. Right. That was the show.

MADGE. Accepted that rejection pretty well, I think. Although I thought I did make it clear that we were only rehearsing. Dissatisfied at the prospect of that being the legacy I leave behind, I decide to have another go the following year. Now, this is why rehearsal is so important. 2003? Merely the dress run. 2004, however, should win all the awards for Best Revival.

Another Christmas production of Cinderella *plays. Madge is a year older and still just as assertive. Far worse, in fact. The players: Madge, Lissy, Mum, Auntie Debby. The audience: Grandma, Great Uncle Stan, Great Auntie Ev. The cameraman: Dad (again).*

8-YEAR-OLD MADGE. Okay! Quiet!

DAD (*from behind the camera*). Don't be bossy.

8-YEAR-OLD MADGE. Three, two, one. Welcome to the show of *Cinderella*.

MUM (*to Lissy who is Cinderella again*). You're supposed to be sweeping up.

8-YEAR-OLD MADGE. NO. Five, four, three, two, one. Start… NO, DON'T START YET. Don't start yet… START. From the first line again.

So many mixed signals. Mum and Auntie Debby are reprising their roles as stepsisters. 8-year-old Madge mouths the words from the wings.

AUNTIE DEBBY/STEPSISTER. 'It's an invitation to a royal ball. The Prince is trying to find a bride.'

8-year-old Madge makes their grand entrance onstage.
They wear a Santa hat and a flowing scarf wrapped
around their neck. The campness is next-level.

8-YEAR-OLD MADGE//FAIRY GODFATHER. 'I am your
Fairy Godfather.'

GREAT UNCLE STAN (*heckling from the audience*). And a
right godfather you make.

8-YEAR-OLD MADGE/FAIRY GODFATHER. Shut up. 'I
am here to grant you a wish.'

COUSIN LISSY/CINDERELLA. 'What wish?'

8-YEAR-OLD MADGE/FAIRY GODFATHER. 'You *will* go
to the ball.'

A close-up of Great Uncle Stan cringing with laughter.

COUSIN LISSY/CINDERELLA. 'How can I? I haven't got
a dress.'

8-YEAR-OLD MADGE/FAIRY GODFATHER. 'Well, *wish.*
Wish, Cinderella.'

The transformation scene takes a while.

GREAT AUNTIE EV. The ball'll be over by the time you get
her there.

8-YEAR-OLD MADGE. Quiet!

At the ball:

DANCE!!

The finale:

(*Leading the company in song.*) OH WHAT FUN IT IS
TO RIDE IN A ONE-HORSE OPEN SLEIGH. HEY!

Curtain call:

(*Screaming.*) ALL GET IN A LINE. GET IN THIS LINE.
MUM, GET IN THIS LINE. Come on. At the end.

Mum is unsure what to do with her sausage roll.

MUUUM DON'T WORRY ABOUT THAT.

MUM. Well, I can't put it on the floor.

Eventually Mum joins the chaotically organised line. All bow.

8-YEAR-OLD MADGE. We hope you enjoyed it.

GRANNY GRIMBLE. Very nice. Very nice. Is that the end now?

No.

8-YEAR-OLD MADGE. They all lived happily ever after and thanks to our…

The Santa hat gets stuck in the scarf. Ruins the moment.

GRANNY GRIMBLE. Watch your mom's scarf.

8-YEAR-OLD MADGE (*recovers the hat*). And thanks to our writer Robert Madge. And our director Robert Madge.

GREAT UNCLE STAN. Who's Robert Madge?

Certificate time. Again.

8-YEAR-OLD MADGE. 'This certificate is presented to…' (*Looks for Mum.*)

She's gone back to her sausage roll.

GET IN THE LINE. '…Janice Madge for playing an excellent part of the second stepsister and trying really hard to put expression into it, not like last year.' And this is the Christmas show on Christmas Eve and WE VERY HOPED YOU ENJOYED IT.

MUM. A round of applause for the director and the playwright! Yay!

As Madge goes to receive their well-earned applause, the Santa hat gets stuck again. Auntie Debby can't hold in her laughter any longer. What a mess. 8-year-old Madge has had enough.

8-YEAR-OLD MADGE. Right. I'm getting my costume off. Have a very merry Christmas and a happy New Year.

GREAT AUNTIE EV. Thank you.

8-YEAR-OLD MADGE. God bless us, everyone.

The video ends on a still of Great Uncle Stan looking dumbfounded.

MADGE. Yeah, same, Uncle Stan. But compare the two. In my opinion, one of the rare instances where the remake improves on the original. My Fairy Godfather? Ten times the performance Marcus gave us the year before. In short, if you want to help your son put on a successful Disney parade, rehearsal is everything. The costumes won't go awry, Peter Pan won't face-plant into the carpet and you won't be asked on a whim to be an owl.

By this point, I've been putting on shows in living rooms across the West Midlands for a good few years and my parents can tell I've exhausted all possible venues on my tour. What next? Where do you go when you peak at Fairy Godfather? Mum and Dad have the common sense to see that my gift deserves to be shared with a wider audience than Auntie Evelyn and Uncle Stan and so they enrol me on a performing-arts programme. Step Five: Stagecoach.

A video compilation from Madge's days at Stagecoach plays, starting with a vocal warm-up and segueing into a rendition of 'Anything Goes'. Madge narrates over the song.

If, like my parents, you haven't a clue what to do with your flamboyant monster of a child, send them somewhere that's full of them. Now, some top training tips for the industry. Always elongate the vowels. (*Demonstrating, as per the video.*) 'Shooock'... 'Rooock'. Will really set you apart in the room. And nearly every casting breakdown asks you to sing in your own accent so, really, I was ahead of the game. (*Sings in a Brummy accent.*) ''STEAD OF LANDING ON PLYMOUTH ROCK.' Next tip. Before any dance break, always warm up. Ideally pick a song you relate to.

We see Stagecoach Madge in a dance warm-up. The
music is 'You're a Superstar' by Love Inc.. They are
bending in the opposite direction to everyone else.

That's it. You bend in that opposite direction, babe. March to
the beat of your own drum.

Everyone else follows the lead of their teacher and does
shoulder-rolls. Stagecoach Madge point-blank refuses.

Yeah, just don't even do the shoulder-rolls. Just don't bother.
All warmed up? Great.

Video cuts back to the 'Anything Goes' dance break.
Whilst most are engaged in a box step, Stagecoach Madge
is preoccupied with their nostrils.

Always time for a cheeky nose-pick.

Stagecoach Madge is visibly bored.

Yeah, if you're not picked to do the tap routine, try not to look
quite so disappointed.

Stagecoach Madge doesn't get to do the tap break, merely
slaps their legs. They are considerably unimpressed.

'Twenty-five quid a week to slap my thighs.'

Stagecoach Madge rubs their eyes.

Ooh – keeping you up?

Song ends.

And button.

Stagecoach Madge awkwardly strikes a final pose.

It's not long before we're delving into some age-appropriate
musical-theatre repertoire.

The Stagecoach kids are performing 'Do You Hear the
People Sing?' from Les Mis.

Sing along if you know the words.

The Stagecoach kids stomp their feet to the music.

Choreo! And march!

The Stagecoach kids awkwardly march. Everyone is gloriously out of time with one another. The video cuts to another Les Mis *number from the Stagecoach performance.*

First ever solo, this. Quite monumental.

STAGECOACH MADGE. 'OW DO YOU DO? MY NAME'S GAVROCHE

Dad lowers the camera. We can no longer see Stagecoach Madge.

MADGE. And then film the floor.

Stagecoach Madge then forgets the words.

Fucked it. One job.

The video cuts sharply to a video of 14-year-old Madge as Gavroche in the Les Misérables in Concert: The 25th Anniversary. *The actual* Les Mis. *The real* Les Mis. *On DVD. Madge feigns modesty, asking the sound desk to stop the video but really wanting the opposite.*

Sorry. I… don't know how that got in there. (*Cher hair-toss. Holds up a fiver. Promises to give it to the sound desk later.*) Thus begins a lifetime of *Les Mis.*

We hear the rousing 'Thénardier Waltz': 'This one's a queer but what can you do?' Madge has opened the fancy-dress box and discovered a flute and a red-and-yellow striped costume.

Tell you what, Eponine's got nothing on my storyline. In this parade, as Belle, I'm going to have to pretend to fall in love with the Beast. We all know last time it was quite tricky for me to play that role convincingly. (*Lip-syncs to 'Belle' in the parade.*)

'I love you, Beast.'

So what I'm going to have to do is to imagine said Beast is someone I really could fall in love with. Substitute Beast with someone I actually fancy. This is acting. Don't worry if it's a bit

– (*Motions 'over the head'*.) It's a complex industry. Now, who better to substitute the Beast with than my very first crush? It's at Stagecoach where this happens.

A happy memory floods into view.

On my eighth summer Stagecoach puts on a musical. It's the story of the Pied Piper. Now, I don't know what it is. It might be his red-and-yellow stripes, it might be his flute, but I fall deeply and madly in love with the Pied Piper of Hamelin. I'm besotted. It's not the first time he's tickled my fancy. He first caught my eye when he played Raoul in the Phantom Megamix. But the flute really confirms my suspicions. I'm a queer! I mean, the clues were there. It started when I was four months old. You see, my Great Auntie Ev was talking about a neighbour's cystoscopy operation over Christmas dinner. The word 'penis' gets mentioned and, as you can see, I'm hooked on this new vocabulary.

A selection of videos, the first taken from Madge's first Christmas.

GREAT AUNTIE EV. The nurse says 'well they do so-and-so and then they put this tube up your penis'.

MUM. That was terrible! Up the penis!

DAD (*making up a song*). EV SAYS PENIS, EV SAYS PENIS.

The camera pans to Baby Madge, who is open-mouthed in awe and fascination.

Look. Robert looks absolutely shocked. Look at him. He looks absolutely shocked.

MUM. I should think he is shocked.

The second, a video of Madge's grandad reading the inscription in his birthday present. It's a book from his old school friends, whom Dad names.

DAD. Jack Gravener. Ray Cox...

9-year-old Madge is suddenly interested.

9-YEAR-OLD MADGE. Cocks?!

And finally, 8-year-old Madge on a Slip'n'Slide.

8-YEAR-OLD MADGE. Who wants to see me swallow a mouthful? Daddy, do you want to see me swallow a mouthful?

DAD. Yeah.

8-YEAR-OLD MADGE. Righty-oh. I'll try my best to impress you.

8-year-old Madge splashes about in the water.

MADGE. My whirlwind romance with the Pied Piper is a short-lived one. Unrequited too. It's hard for an Early Stages to connect with a Stage Three. But even though the relationship clearly isn't viable, I still dream that we might run off together and elope in some distant utopia like Lichfield. I become Audrey, dreaming of a matchbox of our own, gazing wistfully out of my bedroom window.

The set is transformed into a rainbow-filled dream sequence. As this comes to an end, Madge comes across some reports. The rainbow begins to fade.

(*Reading.*) 'Robert is a quiet member of the group who always works hard and tries his best.' That's what the Stagecoach reports say. 'Just a little more confidence needed.' I know what you're thinking – they must have got me mixed up. See, the thing is, Stagecoach coincides with Year 3 of primary school. Not the best of times. Shame really. I was so excited to start as well. Like a precocious little Matilda.

A video of 4-year-old Madge on their first day at school. Dad films, proudly.

DAD. Hello!

4-YEAR-OLD MADGE (*from outside the room*). Hello!

DAD. Come on then. Let's have a look.

4-year-old Madge gingerly enters the living room. They're wearing their school uniform.

Stand there. Right then. Who's a smart boy?

4-YEAR-OLD MADGE. Me.

DAD. Right, and why are you all smart today?

4-YEAR-OLD MADGE. Because I'm going to school.

DAD. You're going to school. So you're a…?

4-YEAR-OLD MADGE. A grown-up!

DAD. A grown-up boy now… It's Tuesday the 9th of January 2001.

MUM. Yeah.

4-YEAR-OLD MADGE. I didn't know it was January!

DAD. Yeah. Do you wanna – do you wanna – do you wanna go and get your, uh – school bag out the hall?

4-YEAR-OLD MADGE. Ooh yes!

DAD. Show us your school bag.

4-year-old Madge potters off to retrieve their school bag. It's all very exciting.

4-YEAR-OLD MADGE. Ooh it's a funny old bag.

The bag is revealed. Mickey Mouse!

DAD. Turn round. Let's have a look at the back. Wow!

4-YEAR-OLD MADGE. Mickey Mouse!

MUM. Son, I've put your Quavers in there if you want them, alright?

MADGE. Believe it or not there are actually parts of my childhood that aren't captured on camera. I know, right? Can you believe it? Like a lot of us I'm sure, school… could be better. Some of the Year 6 lads that don't quite understand how a 'boy' might not be into football and stuff decide to work out their confusion the only way they know how – a cheeky punch at the school gates, you know how it goes. Anyway, after a significant thump behind the bike sheds I finally break the news to Mum and Dad. Well, you give my mum the option of fight or flight and she will fight. She marches right up to that school. 'Hello, I'll be working here now.' She gets some shifts as a dinner lady, watching over me like some kind of hawk in a hairnet. She wants to make sure I'm safe and I do feel safe with her there so I spend lots of time with her, which, shocker, only fuels the fire for the Year 6 lads. 'Only friend's his mum.' So Mum doesn't know what to do so she arranges a meeting with the school to try and get some help. Me and Dad are there too, sinking into our seats. Mum doesn't mince her words. 'So, what are you going to do?' 'Well maybe if your son didn't spend so much time as Cinderella in the imaginative play area, he might make friends.' That's what the teacher says. Words to that effect, at least. Essentially, it's my fault. Now the Year 6 lads are 10. Still kids. Their punches are a bit excusable. But that's the real punch to the stomach. What the teacher says. Just before the summer holidays, I get my report: 'Robert needs to be careful that his dramatic facial expressions don't upset some of his peers, as this will not help him maintain friendships.'

A couple of years before this, my fifth Christmas, I go to the school disco. There's a girl there from Year 4 wearing this Santa hat. But not just any old Santa hat. A Santa hat with plaits. Santa with luscious locks. I grab a Ribena, make my way over. 'Lottie, where did you get your Santa-plaits hat from?' 'Woolworths.' 'Dad, we must go to Woolworths and we must go now. There's a Santa-plaits hat and I simply must have it.'

> *A video of 5-year-old Madge unwrapping a Christmas present. It's the Santa-plaits hat. They wear it with pride, joyfully tossing their wig. And their family don't bat an eyelid. No judgement. Just happiness.*

So, I wear that Santa hat because... well, it makes me happy. Then a few years later, you're told that it shouldn't. So, you stop being Cinderella in the imaginative play area and you stop asking Lottie where she got her Santa-plaits from and you stop doing the shows in the living room because that's not going to help you make friends and then you're the quiet member of the group. Just a little more confidence needed. And that's that.

Song: Pieces of My Heart

ANYTHING IS POSSIBLE BUT ONLY IN YOUR LIVING
   ROOM
YES, ANYTHING IS POSSIBLE – DID I GIVE MYSELF
   AWAY TOO SOON?
ALL MY IMAGINATION
AND STILL THEY SHUT ME OUT
IF ANYTHING IS POSSIBLE
THEN WHY DO I STILL DOUBT?

PACK UP THE SUITCASE AND THE HAT
YOU ARE A BOY. NO USE FOR THAT
PACK UP THE GLITTER, WIG AND DRESS
DIDN'T THEY BRING ME HAPPINESS?
ALL OF THE TREASURES OF MY PAST
SHOULDN'T HAVE THOUGHT THAT IT COULD LAST
SO PACK UP THE HOME-MADE CARTOON ART
PACK UP THE PIECES OF MY HEART

SHOULDN'T HAVE BEEN SO BOLD AT SCHOOL
SHOULDN'T HAVE STOOD UP ON THAT STOOL
BELTING MY HEART OUT, PROUD AND STRONG
WHO KNEW SUCH THINGS COULD BE SO WRONG?

PEOPLE USE WORDS THAT CUT AND STING
THINK OF THE PAIN YOUR WORDS CAN BRING
WHY BE SO CRUEL WHEN YOU COULD SING?
ONE TINY WORD SPOILS EVERYTHING

SO PACK UP THE SUITCASE AND THE HAT
NEVER WILL YOU HAVE USE FOR THAT.
PACK UP THE GLITTER, WIG AND DRESS
THEY BROUGHT ME SO MUCH HAPPINESS
ALL OF THE TREASURES OF MY PAST
I SHOULD HAVE KNOWN IT WOULDN'T LAST
SO PACK UP THE HOME-MADE CARTOON ART
PACK UP THE PIECES OF MY HEART

Song comes to an end.

From this moment, all productions are reserved for the living room and the living room alone. No more singing 'In My Own Little Corner'. Outside of that front door, it's time to do the boy things like football and stuff and sports day. My parents realise it's all been a bit much lately, so we pack our bags and pop to Devon for a holiday. We rent a little caravan on a holiday park and the sea air works wonders so I treat the family to a rare performance.

A video of Chitty Chitty Bang Bang, *performed in a caravan on holiday in Devon.*

11-YEAR-OLD MADGE. LULLABY BAYYY...

Granny Grimble is making sandwiches.

GRANNY GRIMBLE. Jon. One or two slices?

11-YEAR-OLD MADGE. ME OL' BAMBOO, ME OL' BAMBOO, YOU BETTER NEVER BOTHER WITH ME OL' BAMBOO...

Granny Grimble attempts to serve the sandwiches. Gets stuck behind the dance break.

WITH ME OL' BAMBOO, YOU BETTER NEVER BOTHER WITH ME OL' BAMBOO.

The video cuts to Granny Grimble asking all the important questions as 11-year-old Madge changes costume in the bedroom.

GRANNY GRIMBLE. So in the morning – toast for breakfast?

MUM. Yeah.

Granny Grimble tries to remove an uncooperative shelf from the oven.

GRANNY GRIMBLE. Ooh this blooming thing!

Granny Grimble talks us through the evening's dinner options, as 11-year-old Madge emerges from the bedroom, dressed as Truly Scrumptious.

I've got a lot of chicken goujons. I've got quiche. And some corned beef...

11-YEAR-OLD MADGE. Don't film yet!

Attention shifts to 11-year-old Madge again, who is making the Chitty sound effects.

Ch-ch-ch-ch-ch-ch-ch-ch...

GRANNY GRIMBLE. So is it alright if I have this other tin of sardines?

11-year-old Madge frowns at this interruption. Chitty – a stool – sprouts wings – a scarf.

11-YEAR-OLD MADGE/TRULY SCRUMPTIOUS. We're falling! OH YOU PRETTY CHITTY BANG BANG, CHITTY CHITTY BANG BANG. FRIEND CHITTY YOU CHITTY PRETTY CHITTY BANG BANG, FINE FOUR-FENDERED CHITTY CHITTY FRIEND.

GRANNY GRIMBLE. I like all that music.

The scene cuts to 'Truly' singing her song. Granny Grimble dances along in the background.

11-YEAR-OLD MADGE/TRULY SCRUMPTIOUS. TRULY SCRUMPTIOUS. SO BEGUILING, YOU'RE THE ANSWER TO MY WISHES...

Cut to 11-year-old Madge dressed as the Child Catcher.

11-YEAR-OLD MADGE/CHILD CATCHER. KIDDY WIDDY WINKIES. (*Screams.*) COME LITTLE KIDDIES!

'Child Catcher' storms offstage.

GRANNY GRIMBLE. I never know when he's acting and when he's –

MUM. He's not acting. He's in a mood.

'Truly' is back. It's the 'Doll on a Music Box' moment. 11-year-old Madge does the robot.

11-YEAR-OLD MADGE/TRULY SCRUMPTIOUS. YEARNING. YEARNING...

The final number:

11-YEAR-OLD MADGE. AND OUR PRETTY CHITTY BANG BANG CHITTY CHITTY BANG BANG WHAT WE'LL DO. OH YES GO GO! OUR FINE FOUR-FENDERED FRIEND.

The last note is held for ages. Mum has to laugh.

MUM. Oh God.

MADGE. Step Six: If you want to help your son put on a successful Disney parade, be like Granny Grimble. I can't stress how important it is that your star is fed with chicken goujons. She once said, 'Charlie is the unseen star of the video.' I think we now know that role belongs to her. If I have to accredit someone for pulling me out of my rut, it's Granny Grimble. She always did.

We see a clip of the Disney parade. 12-year-old Madge is dressed as Ariel and fuming that there's technical difficulties.

GRANNY GRIMBLE. Come along, Ariel.

12-YEAR-OLD MADGE. I KNOW. THAT'S WHAT I MEAN –

GRANNY GRIMBLE (*interrupting*). HELLOOOO WE'VE HAD A LOVELY DAY.

MADGE. Perfect example. She'd always make everything a lovely day. She just had this instinct for when I'd be about to lose my shit and she'd quickly placate the situation by *making everything nice and wonderful*. It's a technique I need to get better at. But I urge you all, if you're ever faced with a broken bubble gun or technical difficulties or a homophobic arsehole on Twitter, just say, 'WE'VE HAD A LOVELY DAY.' And to any teacher that tells you that you spend too much time as Cinderella in the imaginative play area, 'We've had a lovely day.' So be like Granny Grimble and your child will fly. In a car. It's still the only one I've ever been able to drive.

Madge's attention is drawn to the big tall thing covered by a dust sheet.

I was about to pack this away. But I think you should see it. Granny Grimble was Mum's mum but Dad's parents were alright too because they built me this. Christmas 2004. They dress it up as though we're about to surprise my Auntie Debbie with a present.

> *We see a video, taken from Christmas 2004. All the family are gathered in Nan and Grandad's lounge. Cousins are shushing one another, uncles are waiting expectantly, there's a general air of bottled-up excitement over this gift that's about to be given.*

DAD. Come on then, Robert, bring Debbie in to have a look at it.

GRANDAD. Here y'are, Deb. I hope you like this.

> *8-year-old Madge is guided into the room by Auntie Debbie – another auntie by the name of Debbie, only this time spelt with an 'ie'. Lots of Debs in this family. She's in on the act. 8-year-old Madge is ready to present Debbie with her present. Turns out…*

AUNTIE DEBBIE. What's that?

8-YEAR-OLD MADGE (*awestruck*). It's actually mine.

> *It's a home-made puppet theatre.*

In real time, Madge pulls the dust sheet off the big tall thing. It's the puppet theatre, in all its glory. It really is beautiful, standing at six foot, bedecked with red-velvet curtains. As the video plays, Madge's childhood comes to life.

AUNTIE DEBBIE. Isn't that wicked?

8-YEAR-OLD MADGE. Thank you!

NAN. You know who made you that?

8-YEAR-OLD MADGE. Grandad!

GRANDAD. And in here…

DAD. Watch this, Robert.

GRANDAD. Some little friends for you...

Grandad opens two large boxes, full of dazzling home-made puppets, hand-painted and sewn by Nan and Grandad. Madge is overwhelmed with excitement.

8-YEAR-OLD MADGE. Whoa! It's got all the characters! (*Goes to grab Punch and Judy.*)

DAD. Gently!

AUNTIE DEBBIE. Stand by the theatre.

8-year-old Madge poses for a picture in front of their new theatre.

Oh, that is brilliant.

DAD. You know how long your grandad and nanny have spent on this, Robert? Months and months and months.

8-YEAR-OLD MADGE (*going inside*). Oh wow it's cool!

Grandad teaches 8-year-old Madge how to open and close the tabs.

GRANDAD. Yeah, the white ones – the white ones up here, Robert... Now, pull 'em gently. Not all at once. Just little – No, little tufts... That's it. Like that.

AUNTIE DEBBIE (*as the curtains open*). Here he comes!

GRANDAD. And now the black ones, again –

8-YEAR-OLD MADGE. Are the ones to / bring it back?

GRANDAD. To close it. Now do it gently.

AUNTIE DEBBIE. Oh, he's gonna have hours of fun with this in' he?

GRANDAD (*putting a black cloth over the top*). And this goes over the top to black it all out so they can't see / inside.

8-YEAR-OLD MADGE. A blackout!

Grandad reads aloud the instruction manual he has made to go with it.

GRANDAD. You'll note the clips as you can see… Clips K1 and L14.

NAN. There's pockets there to put your puppets in.

8-YEAR-OLD MADGE. THERE'S POCKET – THERE'S EVEN POCKETS HERE TO PUT THE PUPPETS IN!

AUNTIE DEBBIE. Is there anywhere for a bottle of pop? Is there a cupholder?

A cousin, Ben, stands at the foot of the theatre as though it were a bar.

COUSIN BEN. Can I have a pint please, Robert?

8-YEAR-OLD MADGE. Does anyone wanna come and see the backstage?

Dad and Auntie Debbie have a look backstage.

DAD. Gosh. It's brilliant, Robert.

AUNTIE DEBBIE. Isn't it brilliant.

DAD. You give Nanny and Grandad a big hug for that.

AUNTIE DEBBIE. Are you gonna say thank you to Grandad? Nanny's made all the costumes. She's spent hours sewing. Come and give them a big hug.

8-year-old Madge flings themselves into their nan's arms.

8-YEAR-OLD MADGE. Thank you.

NAN. What did you think when you saw it?

8-YEAR-OLD MADGE. I was thinking 'oh my God'.

AUNTIE DEBBIE. Every time I come down they were painting heads and sewing and…

DAD. I'm chuffed I got that on video.

The calm after the storm.

NAN. And would you like a nice cup of tea?

We hear a voice memo.

DAD (*voice-over*). I can remember – I'd finished work early once and I can remember walking in and your nan literally was whipping something away from you and shoving it into the – like, she had this little pouffe that I sit on now... and I like, looked, I said 'What's that?' and she said nothing and she was smiling, she was saying, 'It's nothing. It's nothing.' I said 'What was it?' She said 'We're just playing. We're just playing.' She said 'I made – ' and it was all plaits.

We see a video of said plaits.

23-YEAR-OLD MADGE (*voice-over*). It was a wool wig.

DAD (*voice-over*). A what?

23-YEAR-OLD MADGE (*voice-over*). A wool wig. She made wigs out of wool.

DAD (*voice-over*). Yeah, it was like cream plaits.

23-YEAR-OLD MADGE (*voice-over*). It was wool, yeah.

DAD (*voice-over*). And Mom was going, 'Oh he loves it. He loves it. And he – he likes all the dressing-up and whatever,' so then I was like, 'Have you got a soldier outfit?' and I think it was like – like – twelve, eighteen months later I bought you the Beast outfit...

We see the Beauty *and the Beast* *video play once more, 6-year-old Madge dressed as the Beast.*

Fucking hell that was expensive... Thinking, 'Oh, well, if he's that way inclined, I can change it with this outfit. Instead of buying him Belle... I'll buy him the Beast.'

23-YEAR-OLD MADGE (*voice-over*). I think there comes a point where you have to just give up because it's too much energy and what you said... what you said to that mother, you said it so simply but it's so true. You said, 'We have to let kids be themselves because then it just makes parenting easy.'

We see a video from Stagecoach. 8-year-old Madge is singing a solo from Mary Poppins. *'Wind's in the east,*

> *there's a mist coming in'. The video cuts to a radio*
> *interview from 2006.*

INTERVIEWER (*voice-over*). The Scissor Sisters it was and 'I Don't Feel Like Dancing'. Well now I've been looking forward to this for some considerable time because with me now is Robert Madge who's currently living a life very few 9 or 10-year-olds would ever dream of because Robert is appearing nightly in London's West End as part of the cast of *Mary Poppins*.

> *A video clip of 9-year-old Madge on* Blue Peter *with the*
> *cast of* Mary Poppins, *performing 'Step in Time'. The*
> *radio interview continues. Madge lip-syncs the following*
> *as though they were a celebrity – shades, hat, scarf,*
> *absolute icon behaviour.*

INTERVIEWER (*voice-over*). It's hard to know where to start talking to you really cos there's so much but tell me first of all, when did you first think that an actor's life was something you'd quite fancy?

9-YEAR-OLD MADGE (*voice-over*). Um. Just… my dad. It – it was down to my dad really cos he got me into doing little shows at home and I really enjoyed them and then I went to Stagecoach and from there I just developed onto it. I just – love it.

INTERVIEWER (*voice-over*). Was there not something else you would sooner have done? Like, you know, playing outside or playing on your computer games or something? <u>Acting?</u>

This catches 9-year-old Madge off-guard.

9-YEAR-OLD MADGE (*voice-over*). Um. I. I'm not – that sort of person. I don't really like football and stuff. I do like riding round my bike occasionally. Like going to uh – the park and stuff. Um. But yeah I think acting's really good.

Madge removes the celeb garb.

MADGE. People always assume because of *MP* – sorry. *Mary Poppins – MP*'s an abbreviation… (*Jazz hands.*) musical theatre. People always assume that because of this, my parents must have been Mama Rose. They weren't. Although Mum was fuming when I didn't go onstage to meet Sooty in the *Goldilocks* panto, not because of what it could have done for my career but because, in her words... (*Lip-syncs to Mum's words*.)

> MUM. You'd have got a free Sooty and Sweep and we had to buy one.

People are baffled when the child actually wants to do it. 'Surely not. Surely you'd want to play outside or play on your computer games.' The parents MUST be pushy. No. There is actually such thing as the pushy child. 'Are you filming?' Besides, some 'boys' aren't interested in playing outside or playing on computer games or football and stuff but we'll try and say what's expected, that we 'ride round on our bike occasionally' in perfect RP because we're trying to get into Sylvia Young's when really we want to say 'I'm too busy dressing up as Winifred Sanderson and putting on parades in my hall to give a shit about your gender stereotypes.' So, the radio thought that theatre couldn't possibly be what a 10-year-old 'boy' would truly want to do. My Disney World journal disagrees:

> *We see stills from said Disney World journal.*

'At Hollywood Studios we went straight into the Villains Shop. I was very disappointed to find out that the Cruella de Vil wigs have vanished into thin air.'

'Went straight into a shop called Outfitters. Was hoping they'd have some queen dresses for CRYSTAL (you know, my sister...).'

'On the way out, guess what I spotted? An Ariel wig! Next time when Mum's here I'll buy it. It'll look a bit strange. Two blokes buying a wig.'

So many of us would have wanted that Ariel wig but it's scary to be different so we'd invent a Crystal, an excuse, it's not for 'him', it's for 'her'. So, next time, when Mum's there, we buy that wig. For 'Crystal'. And she's really good.

*We see a video of 13-year-old Madge dressed as Ariel,
using that same scooter, singing 'Part of Your World'.*

Madge seems to 'break character'.

In 2020, I post this video online. I get a comment from a
mother. She says that her 'beautiful little girl is now an
extremely handsome little boy'. She goes on: 'I'm so so blessed
to have him as my son. He is such a sweetheart with the most
beautiful soul. Unfortunately once we came out to his friends'
parents everyone turned their backs on us. He has absolutely no
friends. It's devastating. We can't ever have birthday parties
because nobody will come. I love my son so so so much.' The
actual lyrics of 'Kill the Beast' aren't really 'ooh his monstrous
appetite'. They are, in fact, 'We don't like what we don't
understand. In fact, it scares us.' I don't think a child turning a
towel into a mermaid tail and using a scooter to represent the
motion of swimming is particularly terrifying. But some people
do. I forgot to mention this bit earlier but I'm a test-tube baby.
Mum and Dad tried for six years. Lots of shit went wrong but
when I eventually decided to turn up after a third round of IVF,
Granny Grimble said this:

*A video of Granny Grimble in the hospital, meeting her
grandson for the first time.*

GRANNY GRIMBLE. I think a baby waits for you, you
know.

MADGE. 'I think a baby waits for you.' Well, it was worth the
wait because I ended up with parents that respond to a mother
who is worried for her child and say:

We see Dad's response.

'If our only duty as parents is to allow our kids to be what they
want to be… then it makes parenting pretty easy in my opinion.'
Some people choose hatred. You can't take that away from
them. They're infected. In the words of Whitney's Fairy
Godmother, 'She can't handle how fabulous you are.' The Year
6 lads, they couldn't handle it, but my mum and dad let me
dance. And when we live in a world full of Year 6 lads, family

support should be the bare minimum. It's easy. And, you know what, even if you don't have a dad that will help you put on a parade in your hall, I will personally take it upon myself to micromanage the entire affair. Speaking of, I think we're about ready to have another go at it.

> *A video of a living-room performance. Granny Grimble is applauding, thinks (or hopes) it's finished.*

GRANNY GRIMBLE. Jolly good.

6-YEAR-OLD MADGE. No, not the end yet.

MUM. *Coronation Street*'s on in a bit.

Don't worry. Mum. I've nearly finished. You can watch *Coronation Street* in a minute. Step Seven: 'My Son's a Queer. What Can I Do?' The burning question that's on everyone's lips. And the answer?

Music begins.

I don't know. Roll with it. There's no handbook. I mean, it's not hard, is it? To love your child. How about we shift the narrative. 'My Son's a Queer, What Can I Do?' 'Your Son's a Queer? I'm Jealous of You.' We bring joy. We bring happiness. And if you choose to miss out on happiness, that's weird. That's the handbook. Happiness.

Song: We Will Be Loved Anyway

WASTE-PAPER BASKETS AND CURTAINS ON RAILS
MAGICALLY TURN INTO NEVER LAND'S SAILS
SO MANY WONDERS FOR YOU TO ACHIEVE
OH, IF YOU BELIEVE

DON'T BE AFRAID IF YOU DON'T UNDERSTAND
THEY WILL FEEL SAFE IF YOU'RE HOLDING THEIR
    HAND
IT DOESN'T TAKE MUCH, JUST A SIMPLE 'I'M HERE'
OH, NO NEED TO FEAR

SO GO TO THE SHOW
DON'T LEAVE IT TOO LATE

FOR SOON THEY WILL GROW
THINK OF THE MAGIC THAT YOU CAN CREATE
THERE'S JOY TO BE HAD
IF YOU CHOOSE TO LOOK
AND EVEN FOR THOSE THAT DECIDE NOT TO STAY
OH, WE WILL BE LOVED ANYWAY

One final video of a living-room performance: The Little
Mermaid, *complete with projections, disco ball, smoke
machine. Father and son dance together as Ariel and
Ursula. Mum and Grandma clap along with glee. For
something so flamboyant, it's a remarkably simple scene.
At its heart, it's a room filled with love. And chaos. But
mostly love.*

The last show I ever did in my living room had projections. If
you're old enough to put together a set design on Windows
Movie Maker, you're probably too old to be performing as Ariel
for your grandma. Fuck it. Be Ariel. Let your child be Ariel. Let
your child be the Fairy Godfather and Peter Pan and an owl.
Because they're not alone. There's a whole community behind
that Settee Curtain. It all starts in your living room and, who
knows, they might grow up with pride and *that's* magic.

*A montage develops of hundreds of childhood
performances from hundreds of queer people, all united,
yet unaware of our bonds. It's a joyful glimpse at the
community that awaits us. A celebration of our brilliance.
A reminder to be proud of who we were, are, and always
will be.*

UNPACK THE SUITCASE AND GET OUT THE HAT
MAKE MAGIC WANDS OUT OF ANY OLD TAT
THROW ALL THAT GLITTER UP HIGH IN THE AIR
OH, AND YOU'LL BE THERE

YOU RAISE YOUR CHILDREN, NOW LET THEM RAISE
    YOU
OPEN YOUR EYES TO A NEW POINT OF VIEW
WE'RE ALL HERE WAITING, YOU WON'T BE ALONE
OH, IT STARTS AT HOME

SO GO TO THE SHOW
DON'T LEAVE IT TOO LATE
FOR SOON THEY WILL GROW
THINK OF THE MAGIC THAT YOU CAN CREATE
THERE'S JOY TO BE HAD
IF YOU CHOOSE TO LOOK
AND EVEN FOR THOSE THAT DECIDE NOT TO STAY
OH, WE WILL BE LOVED ANYWAY

SO GO TO THE SHOW
DON'T LEAVE IT TOO LATE
FOR SOON THEY WILL GROW
THINK OF THE MAGIC THAT YOU CAN CREATE
THERE'S JOY TO BE HAD
IF YOU CHOOSE TO LOOK
AND EVEN FOR THOSE THAT DECIDE NOT TO STAY
OH, WE WILL BE LOVED ANYWAY

A final voice memo.

DAD (*voice-over*). Cos I did me own make-up... with paint. Kid's paint.

23-YEAR-OLD MADGE (*voice-over*). Yeah. It didn't look that high-end to be honest. You weren't Farrah Moan.

DAD (*voice-over*). Which is a bastard to get off. Cos it burns your skin... And that was it then. You just went then. You just went. You just... You know that expression, he took the baton.

23-YEAR-OLD MADGE (*voice-over*). Like a moth to a...a... a... ball?

DAD (*voice-over*)....No... No, you were given the baton and you just ran with it.

23-YEAR-OLD MADGE (*voice-over*). No but I needed the baton passed to me in the first place and not many people – not many dads pass the baton.

The end of the radio interview from 2006.

INTERVIEWER (*voice-over*). I think it's only fair that we play a favourite of yours from the show. Why do you love the finale so much? This is the finale, isn't it?

9-YEAR-OLD MADGE (*voice-over*). Well, this is the last *song*.

INTERVIEWER (*voice-over*). Right.

9-YEAR-OLD MADGE (*voice-over*). It's the one that proves that the children have learned lots because all the characters of the show come and join in and they're all lovely and dancing in the heavens singing a beautiful song.

INTERVIEWER (*voice-over*). Oh, very nice too. And that's why you enjoy it?

9-YEAR-OLD MADGE (*voice-over*). Yes. That's why I enjoy it.

A fanfare that sounds not dissimilar to 'When You Wish Upon a Star.'

A VERY DISNEY-ESQUE VOICE-OVER. And now, the moment you've all been waiting for. RDM Productions present a Disney parade in your house!

Madge recreates the parade. Costumes, props, suitcase floats. It's still chaotic. Probably more so.

> *Dad appears on camera with a bubble gun, Goofy hat donned, looking just as pissed off as he was in 2009. Bert misses his cue, Dad doesn't listen to a word Ariel says, the costumes go awry. And that's exactly how it should be. There is, however, one slight and important improvement: Maleficent appears, in the dress handmade by Granny Grimble. A triumph.*

Song: Anything is Possible (When the Stage is Your Living Room) Reprise

MADGE.
ANYTHING IS POSSIBLE WHEN THE STAGE IS YOUR
  LIVING ROOM
ANYTHING IS POSSIBLE WHEN YOUR LIFE IS LIKE A
  DISNEY CARTOON
USE YOUR IMAGINATION
THERE'S MAGIC UP YOUR SLEEVE
YES, ANYTHING IS POSSIBLE

IF YOU JUST BELIEVE
IF YOU JUST BELIEVE

8-YEAR-OLD MADGE (*voice-over*). WE VERY HOPED YOU ENJOYED IT!

7-YEAR-OLD MADGE (*voice-over*). Right. That was the show.

> *A video of the Little Brummy Child and their parents taking a bow in their living room.*

End.

The Videos

Hello, reader. You made it this far. Congratulations. For your viewing pleasure (and to reassure you that all of this ridiculousness did, in fact, happen – it's not a joke. I know, hard to believe, isn't it?), I thought it might be fun to direct your attention to a few of the videos that feature in the play, or at least, some long-winded URL links to the videos that feature in the play. Type them in. See what happens. (The videos will play. That's what will happen. It's not that exciting really.)

If you've seen them already, welcome home. If this is your first time, prepare yourselves. A stiff drink might be needed to get you through. Enjoy!

My Disney Parade   youtu.be/1SeBoZGoORE

I turned my house into Disneyland   youtu.be/fLVQIT_0w1k

RDM Productions present *Beauty and the Beast*
                                youtu.be/ojuMY0WlcZg

RDM Productions present *Peter Pan*
                                youtu.be/WNYVeePy1tM

RDM Productions present *Hocus Pocus*
                                youtu.be/u2y4qJf92Sc

RDM Productions present *The Wizard of Oz* (a bedtime story)
                                youtu.be/2IGFkBn3vsA

RDM Productions present *Cinderella*
                                youtu.be/bjKjZxKZ5uA

RDM Productions present *Cinderella* (again)
                                youtu.be/I_1a2EvUrCo

RDM Productions present *Chitty Chitty Bang Bang* in a caravan
                                youtu.be/NtaelmnID2Q

RDM Productions present *The Little Mermaid*
(featuring a projector)   youtu.be/qftAC2sPlIQ

Afterword: Curtain Call

Jon & Jan Madge (aka the Parents)

Right. Our turn now. Over the recent period, due to Rob's success, we have hilariously become the attention of lots of people praising us as parents. We think it's important to understand that there is no handbook on parenting. There's no exclusive right way, we certainly aren't experts. We wanted Robert to be happy, to enjoy every moment of their childhood and to aim for nothing but happiness in life. So we cheated really; we encouraged Rob to do what they wanted to do, and be what they wanted to be… it's pretty simple. Sorry if you were after some inspirational gem. All we can offer is an honest account of the trials and tribulations that Rob put us through on a daily basis. Here are just a few of the obstacles we faced.

Dad

I would come home from the pub on a Sunday afternoon to discover our lounge had been transformed into a mini London Palladium, the sofa and chairs all facing toward the window to make room for the stage. The throw had become a fire curtain, the hall was a minefield of props and frocks. My instant thought would be 'Who am I today? Peter Pan? Smee? No… Tinkle Bell!'

Mum

We once had neighbours passing by, expressing concern that our house was on fire. 'Don't be ridiculous!' we said. 'The blue smoke billowing out of the lounge window is part of Cinderella's transformation scene!' Fools.

Dad

In the very early days when I got all the female roles, I once had a friend come to pick me up early for the rugby. I was not a very radiant Snow White, sporting rosy cheeks and blue eyeshadow... but not knowing much about make-up, I'd used Rob's paint set. It eventually came off three days later.

Mum

I would often organise the packing for the annual holiday to Devon; Jon would be fixing bikes to the car, Rob's grandma would be bundling her freshly cooked bacon butties into a cool box, stress levels at peak. Just as we thought we had everything we needed and squeezed everything that could possibly fit into the car, Rob would appear with yet another suitcase, filled with contents such as projector, smoke machine, bubble machine, laser lights, disco ball... you know, all the essentials required for a caravan holiday for four plus a dog.

Those are just some examples of the chaos of the Madge household. We had a lot of fun.

One of Rob's favourite songs as a child was 'Anything Can Happen (If You Let It)' from the musical *Mary Poppins*. As parents, our only advice would be to 'let it happen'. If your child wants it, go with the flow, which will hopefully enable them to be themselves and establish their own unique identity and personality. There is so much in the way of anybody growing up in the LGBTQ+ community already that the sanctuary should always be their home and their family.

When blowing out the candles on their 4th birthday cake, we remember Robert's wish: 'I want to be able to fly!' As a parent, all you ever want for your child is for them to achieve their dreams. In the last twelve months, the love and support Rob has received has given us all so much joy. Thanks to you, they're fulfilling their childhood dream... and *soaring*!

To Dad

YOU'RE

This comes with love
at Christmastime
and hopes to
show you, too,
Some part of all the
pride and love,
In every thought
of you.

Happy Christmas
With Love, Dad

Hope you enjoyed the
show of 'Mary Poppins'

Lots of love on XMAS,
Robert

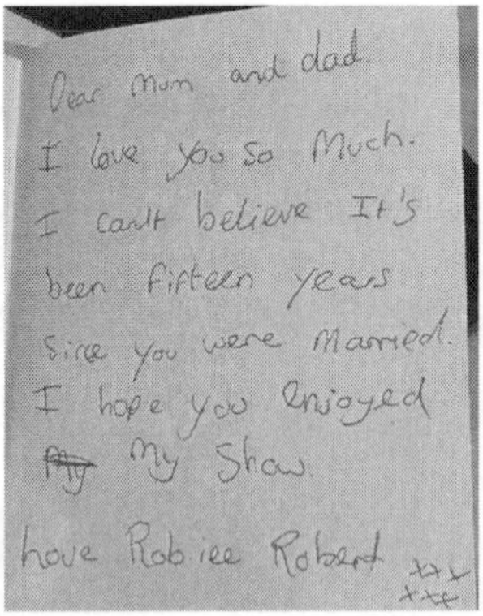
Dear mum and dad.
I love you so Much.
I can't believe It's
been fifteen years
since you were Married.
I hope you enjoyed
my Show.
Love Robiee Robert xxx
xxx

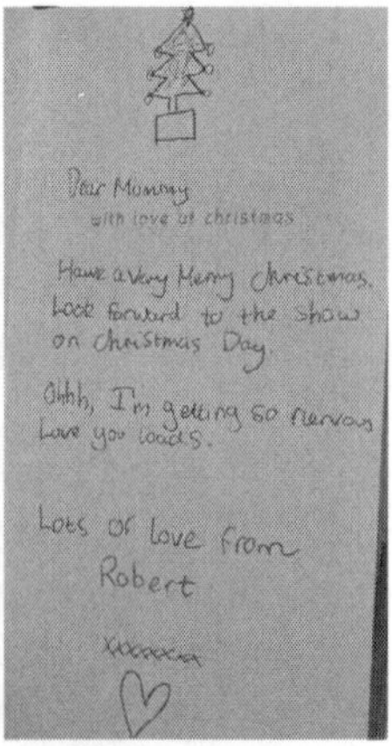
Dear Mommy
with love at christmas

Have a Very Merry Christmas.
Look forward to the show
on christmas Day.

Ohhh, I'm getting so nervous
Love you loads.

Lots of love from
Robert

xxxxxxx

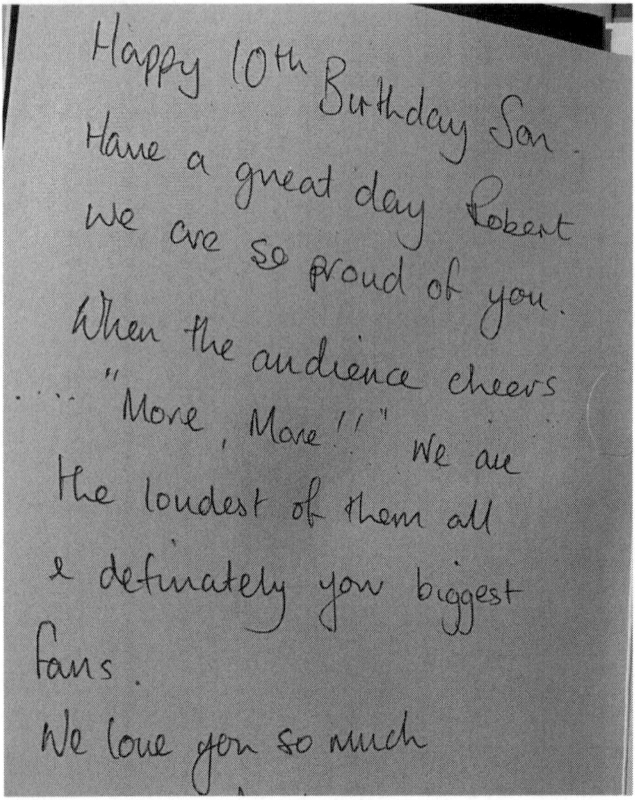
Happy 10th Birthday Son.
Have a great day Robert
we are so proud of you.
When the audience cheers
"More, More!!" we are
the loudest of them all
& definately you biggest
fans.
We love you so much